A PAUSE FOR PEACE

*What God's Gift of the Sabbath
Can Mean to You*

CLIFFORD GOLDSTEIN

Pacific Press Publishing Association
Boise, Idaho
Oshawa, Ontario, Canada

Edited by B. Russell Holt
Designed by Tim Larson
Cover design by Tim Larson
Typeset in 10/11 Times Roman

Unless otherwise indicated, all Scripture quotations
are taken from the New King James Version.
The author assumes responsibility for the accuracy of
quotations cited in this book.

Library of Congress Cataloging-in-Publication Data:

Goldstein, Clifford.
    A pause for peace: what God's gift of the Sabbath can mean
to you / Clifford Goldstein.
        p.   cm.
    ISBN 0-8163-1108-0
    1. Sabbath. 2. Sabbath—Biblical teaching. 3. Seventh-day
Adventists—Doctrines. 4. Adventists—Doctrines. I. Title.
BV125.G65   1992
263'.1—dc20   92-8487
                                                         CIP

92 93 94 95 96 ● 5 4 3

Table of Contents

For
H. E.

Introduction

Two choice words describe my reaction to the book that you hold in your hand—*refreshing* and *exciting*. Refreshing as a cool drink on a hot, thirsty day. And exciting as new and priceless discoveries of neglected truth simply waiting to be uncovered for all the world to see.

The author, a brilliant, young, Jewish Christian writer, will surprise and delight you as he leads you nonjudgmentally through these interesting pages.

I would suggest two questions that will only make keener your desire to proceed. The gospel prophet Isaiah, in his fifty-eighth chapter, verse 12, makes a significant prediction:

> Those from among you
> Shall build the old waste places;
> You shall raise up the foundations of many generations;
> And you shall be called the Repairer of the Breach,
> The Restorer of Streets to Dwell In.

Could this clear statement of God's plan include a restoration of truth lost and confused through the centuries? Does this prediction complement the message of Scripture's last book, Revelation, which describes the recovery of neglected truth as an essential part of last-day events?

The answer to these questions, which follows in these pages, should be for you the unfolding of a thrilling drama—a drama in which you may participate, not simply as a passive bystander, but by becoming totally and happily involved.

And by the way, if there is the slightest doubt that Clifford Goldstein is in touch with your life and mine, his first few words will care for that fear. He ably links an eternally important truth with the suffocating rat race we all attempt to cope with each day. And here is how he does it.

Clifford . . .

George E. Vandeman

PART ONE:

America's Not-So-Secret Sin

1

"It is," wrote one pastor, "the American bargain-basement sin, on sale in virtually every American church."[1]

After a cavernous yawn, an elastic stretch, and a rub of the eyes, evangelical Christians are awakening to their most blatant sin, but only after it has threatened to devastate them, their families, churches, and nation. Despite the biblical commandment, this sin has been so rampant, so entrenched, and so common that it hardly seems wrong.

It is one reason, too, why divorce, alienation, abuse, stress, and loneliness have almost defaced the image of Christ in many Christian families. The damage surfaces, for instance, when parents ceaselessly work to provide material things for themselves and for their children, until they see less of their children than does the baby sitter or teacher. Ironically, the children don't want the teacher, the baby sitter, or even what the parents buy; they want their parents instead.

Because of this sin, someone is always at work or at the store or doing something—until the average American father spends just thirty-seven seconds a day in one-to-one interaction with each of his kids. *Thirty-seven seconds!* Such neglect can produce only a legacy of angry, damaged children whose personalities will become gnarled into angry, damaged adults. Multiply this situation—and worse ones—by thousands, even millions, and we have a church, a faith, a nation in trouble.

Our lives, says Scripture, are to be "hidden with Christ in God" (Colossians 3:3), but often they seem hidden only in ourselves, apart even from our spouses, much less Christ. The Lord used marriage to exemplify the intimate relationship that He seeks between Himself and His church, but this sin has left spouses without the necessary time to maintain the intimacy so crucial to marriage. Couples drift so far apart that the distance brings down home upon their heads.

Also, if spouses don't have time to build an enduring relationship between each other, what about their connection to Christ? If Christian marriage reflects the church's relationship to Jesus, then our marriages aren't the only things in trouble. When Gallup polls show that saints have little less hesitancy to lie, cheat, or steal than sinners, our faith is as flawed as our families. " 'This is eternal life,' " Jesus said, " 'that they may know You, the only true God, and Jesus Christ whom You have sent' " (John 17:3). If we can't take time to know our spouses, how can we know the Lord?

To protect against these problems, Jesus issued a commandment designed to give Christians time for both family and for Himself. Yet because it is so widely broken, most of us don't have time for either.

Too bad, because all believers are aware of this commandment, the remedy for many heartaches, but they have neglected it anyway. And now, in a harvest of abundant bitterness, they are reaping what they've sown by this gross indulgence of Christianity's not-so-secret sin.

Christians *have* the answer, have had it for almost two thousand years. If only they adhered to it!

More and more are.

2

A few years ago, in an attempt to discern reader concerns, the influential evangelical magazine, *Christianity Today*, mailed a survey to 475 random subscribers asking them to rate their interest in such questions about the Christian faith as: "Will a just God really condemn people to hell who have never heard of Jesus?" or "How can I be certain I will go to heaven?"

The results surprised the editors. The question rated of highest concern was, "Should Christians take their Sabbath/Sunday observances more seriously?"

Should Christians take their Sabbath/Sunday observances more seriously? Christians in America haven't taken Sabbath/Sunday observance seriously since the days when citizens could be flogged and then locked in the stocks for desecrating the Lord's Day. With the exception of a few hours in the morning for church, Sunday is usually consecrated to doing what we didn't have time to do the rest of the week, except in the fall, when the day is "set apart" for football. Most Christians expend more effort for Halloween than for Sabbath.

What the *Christianity Today* survey shows, however, is that believers now realize that something is wrong with how they practice their religion. Something is wrong when their faith can't keep their families together, their children off drugs, or the pews filled—and part of what's wrong, they now see, is disregard of the Sabbath commandment.

"Whether or not people keep the Sabbath holy is not an incidental or insignificant matter," writes Baptist preacher Walter

Chantry in his new book, *Call the Sabbath a Delight.* "When God issued this fourth commandment he understood humanity much better than we do. Failure to practice this moral law is a root cause of moral decline, social disorder, and widespread human suffering. No successful recovery of mankind can be devised without the inclusion of the fourth commandment in the remedy."[2]

Chantry's book is one of many pumped off Christian presses in recent years about the "forgotten commandment." More and more evangelicals are aware that they hurt themselves, their families, their churches, and their communities by Sabbath breaking. As one preacher expressed it: "There's a penalty for planting and hoeing corn on Sunday, but it doesn't show in the corn; it shows in the person."[3]

Besides Chantry, others are writing about the importance of the Sabbath. Marva J. Dawn has written the popular book, *Keeping the Sabbath Wholly.* Tilden Edwards's *Sabbath Time: Understanding and Practice for Contemporary Christians* came out in 1982. In 1987, Karen Mains published *Making Sunday Special.* The Lord's Day Alliance, that lone voice crying in the wilderness of Protestant Sunday neglect, published *The Lord's Day* in celebration of its hundredth anniversary. And Pope John Paul II, in his encyclical *Centesimus Annus*, has stressed the need to keep Sunday holy.

Though these people differ in approach, style, and theology, Chantry summarized the basic message: "It is impossible to conceive of any measure more perfectly designed than Sabbath to bring everlasting blessing to individual families, churches and communities. Spiritual men bemoan lack of time to pray, read, worship, witness, teach children. God in His wisdom and grace has provided just such time for these very wishes of the godly by commanding that a day in each seven be set aside, devoted to the Lord."

That day is called Sabbath, and God commands Christians to keep it.

3

Of course, some Christians have been keeping the Sabbath for years, even decades.

"To all who receive the Sabbath as a sign of Christ's creative and redeeming power," says a Seventh-day Adventist book written in the 1800s, "it will be a delight. Seeing Christ in it, they delight themselves in Him. The Sabbath points them to the works of creation as an evidence of His mighty power in redemption. While it calls to mind the lost peace of Eden, it tells of peace restored through the Saviour. And every object in nature repeats His invitation, 'Come unto Me, all ye that labor and are heavy-laden, and I will give you rest.' Matt. 11:28."[4]

In the same century, speaking for the church that formalized Sunday keeping in Christianity, Cardinal James Gibbons wrote: "The institution of the Sabbath [Sunday] has contributed more to the peace and good order of nations than could be accomplished by standing armies and the best organized police force."[5]

James P. Wesberry, executive director of the Lord's Day Alliance, said: "The Lord's Day is the axis upon which our nation turns. What would America do without the Sabbath Day? Our nation is great because of its great preachers and churches, but is great also because it has not forgotten to remember the Sabbath Day to keep it holy."[6]

Obviously, knowledge of the Sabbath blessing is not new, but the growing interest about it among Christians is. This surging consciousness about the day of rest raises questions. Why keep Sabbath? What is the experience of Sabbath keeping? Which is the Sabbath day, Saturday or Sunday? Does it matter? Did Jesus or the apostles change the day to Sunday? Can we keep whatever day we want? How does one keep the Sabbath? What are the benefits of setting aside one day a week?

Of course, whatever conclusions we draw, some will disagree. Which is fine. This book presents one perspective. If the Spirit impresses you that something you learn here is truth, then praise the Lord, who gives wisdom "to all liberally and without reproach" (James 1:5). If not, we are not to judge, but to love one another, "for love is of God; and everyone who loves is born of God and knows God" (1 John 4:7).

For the Sabbath, without love, is not holy, no matter what day one keeps.

PART TWO:

The Sabbath Experience

4

Sabbath is as deep as the day is long (excuse the pun.) It exudes soteriological, eschatological, and ontological messages that theologians have analyzed, debated, and parsed on everything from papyri plucked out of ancient swamps to word processors assembled in Silicon Valley. But Sabbath is also an experience, and until we experience it ourselves, we can't understand the esoteric truths behind it.

It's like the gospel. Excessive theologies have been developed about salvation, but until a person has a born-again experience, until he understands his sin in light of the cross, until he experiences Christ as the only remedy for that sin, the gospel will remain for him nothing but someone else's religious beliefs— boring and not his business.

"How can a man be born when he is old?" asked Nicodemus, a leader in Israel. "Can he enter a second time into his mother's womb?" (John 3:4). Despite all his religious training, Nicodemus hadn't yet been converted, so he remained ignorant of the most basic fact about salvation. He needed to be born again before he, even with all his degrees, could grasp its theology.

When Paul said, "Having been justified by faith, we have peace with God through our Lord Jesus Christ" (Romans 5:1), he wasn't just stating a theological conclusion drawn from Bible study, but a reality that he had *experienced* through Jesus Christ. Only after he had his life-shattering encounter with Jesus did Paul understand justification and know the peace it delivers.

While his countrymen still sacrificed bulls and goats in services holding no more religious significance than butchery in a slaughterhouse, Paul saw Jesus as the fulfillment of those sacrifices because he had an experience with Christ that revealed to him their true meaning. Many with the same training as Paul sought acceptance with God through strict adherence to forms and ceremonies, but Paul knew that acceptance comes only through faith in Christ because his experience had revealed to him the theology behind those forms and ceremonies. And while many Israelites earnestly anticipated the consummation of the Messianic predictions, Paul saw their fulfillment in Jesus because of his experience with Him.

Of course, theology lends itself to the moment, helping us understand our experiences. After the Damascus road, Paul studied the Bible and saw that Jesus indeed fulfilled the prophecies concerning the Messiah as symbolized in the sacrificial system. The Bible confirmed, even helped him understand, his experience. Faith needs both experience and theology, each to enhance, verify, and strengthen the other. Theology, without experience, can lead to cold, dead formalism; experience, without theology, can lead to fanaticism and confusion.

It's the same with the Sabbath. The Bible tells us to "call the Sabbath a delight" (Isaiah 58:13), but how can we unless we experience it ourselves? Theology alone won't do it. Only by an experience of the day, framed in the theology of the idea, can a person delight in the command.

5

When the sun dips on Friday night, pulling Sabbath over my home, and I kneel in prayer, family at my side, it can be a powerful spiritual experience. As we kneel, Sabbath shadows deepening along the walls, how natural it becomes to think back to the first Sabbath, the one God kept at Creation. "And on the seventh day God ended His work which He had done, and He rested on the seventh day from all His work which He had done" (Genesis 2:2). *And now, thousands of years later, I rest on the same Sabbath that God Himself rested on at the creation of the world!* The span of millennia separating us from Eden seems momentarily, mystically bridged. Creation week is no longer just a remote, cosmological event, but the only reason for my own existence at this moment.

Never, except as Sabbath begins, am I more aware that I am a being created by God, an awareness that instantly leads me to my Creator, Jesus. On Sabbath, everything about Jesus comes into sharper focus, because all that can get in the way—the boss, the bills, the broken faucet—are, ideally, removed by the Sabbath, which streams in the window and carries them off for twenty-four hours.

Today, so many souls wander without purpose, without hope, without God, in an existence without promise or future. How can anyone know where he is going if he doesn't know who he is or from where he came? If we originally crawled out of a slime pit, where else can we ultimately wind up but back in one? So why bother with the bitterness, disappointment, and suffering in between? How much dignity can we have, or deserve, merely as creatures with no reason for being except chance? No wonder so many live in frantic dread, for what could be more dreadful than to confront your own meaninglessness?

God wants every human to know that he or she is not meaningless, but that each of us came directly from Him, made in His image, sons and daughters of the King of the universe—and He set aside a special time every seventh day to help remind us.

George Elliott expressed it beautifully: "Against atheism, which denies the existence of a personal God; against materialism, which denies that this visible universe has its roots in the unseen; and against secularism, which denies the need to worship, the Sabbath is an eternal witness. It symbolically commemorates that creative power which spoke all things into being, the wisdom which ordered their adaptations and harmony, and the love which made, as well as pronounced, all 'very good.' It is set as the perpetual guardian of man against that spiritual infirmity which has everywhere led him to a denial of the God who made him, or to the degradation of that God into a creature made with his own hands."[7]

Sabbath is a weekly call home, a weekly reminder that we are God's creatures, first by creation, and then by redemption, beings of inestimable value because we were "bought at a price" (1 Corinthians 7:23), even "the precious blood of Christ" (1 Peter 1:19). By pointing us back to where we came from (God), the Sabbath shows us not only who we are (beings made in the image of that God), but ultimately where we are going (to a world recreated by that God). The Sabbath experience gives life clear direction and purpose because it brings us closer to Jesus Christ, in whom "we live and move and have our being" (Acts 17:28). No wonder that Norman Vincent Peale, reminiscing on his Sabbath experience as a child in turn-of-the-century America, wrote: "Sundays were where life got its meaning and purpose."[8]

Only by keeping Sabbath can one *experience* just how primal, basic, and important the day is to faith in Jesus, an experience that theological treatises and proof texts alone can never produce. Only by keeping Sabbath ourselves can we experience how it enhances our relationship with Jesus. Only by keeping Sabbath ourselves can we experience the joy and wonder of the day. And only by keeping Sabbath can we truly understand the Lord's words that "the Sabbath was made for man" (Mark 2:27).

6

"Come to Me," Jesus said, "all you who labor and are heavy laden, and I will give you rest" (Matthew 11:28). Jesus gives us rest in numerous ways. And one, unquestionably, is the Sabbath day.

Marva J. Dawn, in her intensely personal *Keeping the Sabbath Wholly*, exemplifies one way Jesus, through the Sabbath, gave her rest. In her Ph.D. program she needed to learn Latin, French, and German, all at once. "The only way for me to keep the three languages straight," she writes, "was to devise an arduous study schedule beginning each morning at six." She would study one language, then another, go to class, then return home and study another language until eleven at night, when "I dropped into bed utterly exhausted." The intense pace was necessary, she says, because, "after only six weeks of class, I had to be able to translate a thousand words in a two-hour test in each language."

She feels that she was able to keep following this punishing schedule only because of her "anticipation, celebration, and re-membrance of the Sabbath. Toward the end of the week, the knowledge of that Sabbath would soon give me incredibly powerful comfort and courage to persist, even as, at the beginning of the week, memories of the Sabbath delight I had just experienced motivated me to begin again. . . . Rarely have I experienced such vast relief in the Sunday ceasing from work as I did that summer."[9] Through the blessings of the Sabbath, Marva—burdened and heavy laden—experienced rest in Christ.

One winter, I planted trees in southern Alabama. On my back

I lugged a sackful of baby pines, each the size of a flower. After heaving my pickax into the ground, I would bend down, plant a pine, and then kick in the dirt, repeating the motion hundreds, maybe thousands, of times a day. Our crew began at first light, planting on hills, along ravines, pushing through prickly brush and twisted brambles, throwing the pickax, bending and planting and kicking until dusk, when we would return to camp and collapse. Never with such delight and desire did I anticipate my Sabbath rest. Never were twenty-four hours so precious, so meaningful, so needed.

Friday afternoon, I stopped hours before sundown, during which I prepared for the Sabbath so that when it arrived, instead of doing the laundry or the shopping or any other "work," I was resting, enjoying the Sabbath and experiencing the spiritual realities of this sacred time.

And one of those realities, I then understood, was that the Sabbath protects us from ourselves. Despite the exhausting work, I wrestled with the temptation to plant day after day without a break in order to earn more money. How many people work ceaselessly for material things only to burn themselves out until they can't enjoy them? How many allow themselves to be so enticed with the acquisition of wealth that they become slaves of objects, trapped in the lust of their own greed?

But the Sabbath comes, a weekly break in a vicious cycle that could swallow us in our own avarice. "The Sabbath rest promotes freedom from greed," wrote Christian scholar Samuele Bacchiocchi. "The Sabbath teaches the greedy heart to be grateful—to stop for one day looking for more [things], and start instead gratefully to acknowledge the blessings received."[10]

Rabbi Abraham Joshua Heschel understood this principle. For him the Sabbath sets men free not only from "the tyranny of space," but from covetousness, which is why he linked the fourth commandment, the Sabbath, to the tenth, the prohibition against coveting. "We know," he wrote, "that passion cannot be vanquished by decree. The tenth injunction would, therefore, be practically futile, were it not for the commandment regarding the Sabbath to which a third of the text of the Decalogue is devoted, and which is the epitome of all other commandments."[11]

Perhaps, because of the inherent selfishness that boils in us, the Lord *orders* us to keep the Sabbath, which weekly cools the brew within. In spite of God's command, few keep Sabbath now; if it were optional, no one would. We're too selfish, too desirous of feeding the greedy demons that dwell within. So God orders us to keep Sabbath, just as He orders us not to commit adultery. With so many lessons about greed lost to Christians because the day is ignored, no wonder so many greedy, covetous tares are mixed with wheat in the church.

Once a week, God commands us to stop working, to stop acquiring wealth, to stop reaching for material things—and reach for the spiritual instead. Carnal hearts don't like their money-making interrupted, and perhaps this is a major reason for the rampant Sabbath desecration in American Christianity. We want what we see in the store window; we want it now; and one day out of seven to stop reaching for it seems too much.

But, by stepping out in faith and keeping the fourth commandment, we can be free from the greed that poisons our relationship with others and with God. This is an experience that no pastor or seminary professor can ever give; we must experience that weekly liberation ourselves, that weekly calm, that weekly peace of knowing that we can rest now, that things can wait. Despite all the retorts about "freedom in Christ" used as excuses against Sabbath keeping—in reality, obedience to the fourth commandment frees us, while transgression wraps us in bonds.

"Whoever," Jesus said, "commits sin is a slave of sin" (John 8:34)—Sabbath breakers included. Yet Jesus came to free us, and "if the Son makes you free, you shall be free indeed" (John 8:36). Sabbath remains not only a symbol of that freedom in Christ but a practical way to experience it.

7

At a dinner one evening with Christians, I lamented that two blessings given to us in Eden—marriage and the seventh-day Sabbath—have been desecrated, not only by the world, but by the church. Instantly a young woman at the table, upset with my comment about Sabbath, retorted, "We are now free in Christ."

What does Sabbath breaking have to do with being free in Christ? Somehow, disobedience to the fourth commandment has become the universal symbol of Christian liberty, when disobedience to any of the other nine, such as adultery or murder, is labeled sin.

Her reaction shows that Christians have not yet separated the biblical command to keep the Sabbath holy from the legalistic, pharisaical yoke that ruined Sabbath keeping two thousand years ago. Jesus broke the yoke, not the Sabbath. Why do we reject the Sabbath today merely because people abused it in the past? It's like refusing to visit a doctor today because centuries ago physicians prescribed tobacco for lung ailments.

This reflexive linkage of the fourth commandment to legalism is especially unfortunate because of all the Ten Commandments, none is as well designed as the fourth to give Christians the fullest expression of freedom in Christ. The Sabbath opens to the believer one of the most liberating aspects of the gospel. Far from being a yoke of bondage, Sabbath keeping is a weekly insignia of the emancipation that only Christ provides.

First, at least one day a week, Sabbath guarantees us a break from the burden of the bills, the hassles with the boss, the frustrations of needed repairs. When Sabbath begins, it sweeps over us like a magnet, snatching the secular nuts and bolts of daily life and carrying them off for twenty-four hours, leaving our souls light, easy, free to concentrate on God alone. No other commandment does the same.

In true Sabbath keeping, we are so free and secure in Christ that we can put aside the secular for twenty-four hours and pursue the spiritual instead. By keeping the Sabbath we express that we are in the world but not of it, because for that day, we can tune out the world and tune in God. Sabbath keeping shows that we are not so trapped by the mundane, that it doesn't have such a grip on us, that we cannot weekly slip away from it to spend quality time with Christ. Adherence to the fourth commandment reveals that we have enough trust in Jesus to temporarily suspend our ambitions (though others around us forge ahead) and rest in Christ, enjoying the freedom that comes from faith that God will provide.

What other commandment allows us a weekly respite from the worldly things of our existence? What other commandment opens to us the opportunity to delight in God for twenty-four hours with no secular interruptions allowed? What other commandment gives us the freedom to say, "I am God's, first by creation and then by redemption, and for an entire day I am going to rejoice in my creation and redemption?"

Those enjoying Sabbath experience a freedom in Christ that those ignoring it can never have. Only when we are "doing Sabbath" can we know the pleasures, the liberation, the satisfactions that suffuse it. When we keep the Sabbath, we experience for ourselves the precious gift that God has given to mankind in this day. Sabbath is a powerful, practical way to understand God's tender regard for His creation; keeping it as He commanded can only increase our love for Him as we rejoice in the freedom that He channels to us via the Sabbath.

"What an amazing divine concern the Sabbath rest reveals!" wrote Samuele Bacchiocchi. "It epitomizes God's care and plan for human freedom: freedom from the tyranny of work; freedom from pitiless human exploitation; freedom from over-attachment to things and people; freedom from insatiable greediness; freedom to enjoy God's blessings on the Sabbath in order to be sent forth into a new week with renewed zest and strength."[12]

Swiss theologian Karl Barth stated that "to observe the holy day means also to keep oneself free for participation in the praise and worship and witness and proclamation of God in His congregation, in common thanksgiving and intercession. And the blessing and profit of the holy day definitely depends also on the positive use of this freedom."[13]

Those who ask "But what about all the things that we can't do on Sabbath?" have never kept it properly because those who have know that the question is not "What can't we do?" but "What has God freed us from doing?"

A simple example of this freedom deals with my newspaper. Six mornings a week I pick up the *Washington Post* from my front lawn, and during breakfast I get my fill of war, murder, and scandal along with my cereal. But the seventh morning is the Sabbath of the Lord my God, and on it my soul rests from all the crime, drug busts, and wars. On the holy Sabbath, all the news of the day remains folded in the paper wrapper, while whatever words my eyes take in deal only with salvation, with Jesus, with the wonderful works of God among the children of men. It's a small point, this matter of the morning paper, but it epitomizes an important principle of Sabbath keeping. Multiply this aspect with numerous other "little" ones, and we understand how Sabbath frees us for a greater experience with the Lord.

God knows that we have important tasks, which is why He gives us six out of seven days each week to do them. We can accomplish only so much in one day, and some things have to give way for others. How often during the week are plans to spend extra time in prayer, Bible study, or even ministry pushed aside for more earthly considerations? Sabbath is the one day that protects us from those interruptions, from everything that can hinder our communion with Jesus. Thus, instead of a yoke of bondage, the Sabbath is a day of delight, of freedom—a day set apart especially to be with the Lord. Perhaps that's why it's called the Lord's Day, because the Lord came to set us free, and we can experience that freedom best on His holy Sabbath day.

8

"Now ask the beasts, and they will teach you; and the birds of the air, and they will tell you; or speak to the earth, and it will teach you; and the fish of the sea will explain to you. Who among all these does not know that the hand of the Lord has done this, in whose hand is the life of every living thing, and the breath of all mankind?" (Job 12:7-10).

We don't have to speak to the hills or ask the trout, the cardinals, or the cows. Their words come without prodding. Whether by the prose of land, the verse of beasts, or the song of rivers, nature announces to all mankind that the "hand of the Lord has done this."

Christians worship the Lord Jesus because He "made heaven and earth, the sea and springs of water" (Revelation 14:7). God speaks ceaselessly through His creation, proclaiming that the "things which are seen were not made of things which do appear" (Hebrews 11:3, KJV). So articulate is the heavenly message that "there is no speech nor language where their voice is not heard" (Psalm 19:3). The wonders of nature so explicitly pronounce the existence of God that, according to the apostle Paul, even heathen who never heard of the Lord will be "without excuse" on judgment day because "since the creation of the world His invisible attributes are clearly seen, being understood by the things that are made, even His eternal power and Godhead" (Romans 1:20).

The Lord wants us to learn about Him through the marvels of what He has created and, of all the commandments, only the fourth offers this opportunity. The essence of the commandment

30

itself, by pointing to Creation, calls us to reflect on God's created works, while the practice of the day gives us the time to do it.

In the early 1980s, after having just had a dramatic born-again experience,[14] I lived in rural Georgia in a valley near the southern tip of the Appalachian Trail. On Sabbaths, when I was free, I used to climb over a fence and walk along a dirt road lined on each side by a thin row of trees tangled in wild raspberry bushes. Soon the trees and raspberries stopped, and the road opened into a field of purple and yellow flowers that glistened in the sun, which bathed us in streams of warm light tempered by breezes cascading down the mountains. The mountains themselves formed a wall of trees and cliffs bordered by a sapphire sky, while a creek cut across the field and disappeared into the woods that climbed up the side of the mountain. Here, in this field on Sabbath (which was the only reason I could get away), I had some of my deepest, closest experiences with the Lord.

On those Sabbaths, standing in that field of purple flowers, I first began to know the Lord personally. Putting aside all theology and, rationally, empirically, taking in the scene, my heart burned with the irrefutable realization that not only did God exist, but that He was loving and merciful. Only a loving, merciful God would create the miracles that surrounded me.

Sometimes I would sit in the field, lazy cows resting nearby, and as my eyes and ears greedily sucked in the light and sounds, I was astonished that I could have gone so many years and not known God when His existence now appeared so obvious. *How could I have been so blind?* So often, sharing the field with the cows, I praised the God who had created and redeemed me while the birds punctuated my worship with a background chorus. At times, the presence of Jesus was so real, His closeness so apparent, that I could feel His angels ministering to me.

One time, walking in the field, still a new believer, shadows from sporadic clouds splashing me in cool air, I thought: *O God, I love You. I want to serve You because what I see proves You are good. But how do I know that I am really serving You, the God who created all this? I want to serve and worship that God alone. How do I really, really know?*

Instantly, the answer came. *Sabbath!*

Of course! How obvious! Because this commandment specifically points to the Lord as the Creator, those who keep it acknowledge that they are worshiping that Creator, not anything or anybody else. The Sabbath exists only because the Lord made it to call attention to Himself as the Maker of the world. It's blatant weekly evidence that we worship the true God, who indeed made " 'heaven and earth, the sea and springs of water' " (Revelation 14:7). The realization was so simple, yet so profound, I trembled.

Another Sabbath, walking along that same dirt road, I was praying fervently, and the presence of Jesus seemed especially near. I looked up into the sky, which burned radiantly as if the heavens had opened and the glory of God streamed out in showers of light. Overwhelmed by this powerful revelation of God's holiness, righteousness, and majesty, I dropped to my knees and prayed.

Never before had I realized my own sinfulness and wretchedness. Never had I seen just how great was the gap between myself and God. Never had I understood the futility of every work done by sinful, polluted people like myself. Crushed by my own sin, which seemed so black contrasted against this powerful manifestation of God's glory, I cried out inside, *O God, how can You accept me?* Before the thought ended, the answer flashed across my mind: the cross.

I had understood justification by faith. I had read and accepted all the verses about Christ's death and what it accomplished. I had known that Christ died as the perfect substitute for my sins and that I could be forgiven and accepted only by faith in His sacrifice as my legal substitute. I had known all these things, believed all these things, could preach all these things. But on that Sabbath afternoon, for the first time I experienced the true depth of my own depravity and my own utter helplessness to do anything about it myself. And yet, as a result of that painful realization, I also experienced what it meant to need and have a Saviour.

When I opened my eyes and walked away, I *knew* that works would never save me. Those who think works can save don't know Jesus. They have never glimpsed His holiness or His glory; otherwise, they would understand that anything they do can no more justify them before God than the blood of pigs can wash away their sins. Justification by faith was no longer just theology; it had now become the foundation experience of my whole walk with Christ.

How ironic, too, that I am accused of legalism because I keep the Sabbath, when it was through keeping it that I first learned the futility of legalism. On Sabbath I learned that I could cease from my own works and rest in Christ's works for me. On that afternoon, the Sabbath sun cast the shadow of the cross across my path as never before, and all I could do was fall at the foot of Calvary, cringe at my evil, and rejoice in the goodness of God.

9

Besides all its deep theological ramifications, or even its experiential heavenly pleasures, the Sabbath serves one nitty-gritty earthly function: it gives the family time to be together, and in today's hectic, fast-paced society, that benefit alone makes the day precious. Now more than ever, as the family faces pressures that leave millions of homes tattered, disheveled, and vulnerable, we need every possible protection, and the Sabbath is one of the best because it comes to man from heaven via the Garden of Eden. If God thought that man in Paradise, even before sin, needed the Sabbath, how much more do we need it today?

Of course, Sabbath keeping, even done right, does not guarantee a happy home, a solid marriage, or Spirit-filled children partaking of their parents' faith. Instead, it guarantees only that the family will spend the minimal amount of *quality* time together without which almost no chance exists for a happy home, a solid marriage, and Spirit-filled children. Sabbath doesn't hold within its special twenty-four hours magical promises to idealize family life; rather, it holds practical promises to give families the precious time together to seek that ideal.

Also, if what we become as adults depends so much upon our childhood, how crucial that parents spend the necessary time with their little ones needed to mold characters that will make them useful citizens here and in heaven. Of all the commandments, Sabbath alone gives us that precious time.

With two small children in my own family, I have seen what rich blessings Sabbath carries within its wings. How I wish all homes would take shelter under those heavenly plumes! No one would ever be sorry that he obeyed that commandment; on the contrary, he, too, would sing, "This is the day which the Lord has made; we will rejoice and be glad in it" (Psalm 118:24).

The Sabbath strengthens our family in numerous ways. First, my wife's job is raising the kids, which, however important, doesn't pay the bills. Therefore, I do freelance writing at home (such as this book). As someone who prefers writing even to eating, I write every possible spare minute, except on Sabbath, when my word processor stays off, and I spend all that time with my wife and children. If I didn't keep the Sabbath, I would write then too, much to the detriment of myself (who needs a break) and of my family (who needs time with me). I have learned why God didn't make Sabbath keeping any more optional than He did the commandment against adultery. Instead, He commands us to "keep the commandments of the Lord . . . which I command you today *for your good*" (Deuteronomy 10:13, emphasis supplied).

It's not simply the time together with the family that makes Sabbath special (after all, you can be sick at home for two weeks and be with the family), but it is what we do with this time that gives Sabbath its cutting edge. Because the Sabbath, ideally, carries away secular concerns and worries, our family can enjoy the freedom of uninterrupted interaction and intimacy. No one is working late, writing, at the store, mowing the lawn, or painting the roof. Instead, we are praying, eating, laughing, and walking *together as a family*.

I love to walk with my boy through the wooded trails where we live. We can take our time and enjoy what we see because there's no rush to meet business appointments or to turn on the word processor. Nothing secular is allowed to intrude. My two-year-old son loves to run and yell and laugh and collect sticks and rocks and fallen apples. The richest, happiest, most precious moments of my existence have been on Sabbath afternoons, when I have the freedom to frolic leisurely with my son. Few sounds touch my heart more than his uninhibited shrieks and laughter as he romps free like a little lamb. Sabbath gives us a sacred break, valued beyond money.

My wife and I seek to make the Sabbath unique, a delightful

day that the whole family joyfully anticipates. We want our children to grow up, not abhorring the day as some rigid law that they have to keep in order to go to heaven, but as a time to celebrate the promise of heaven by tasting it now, a time to rejoice in the wonders of God's creation by enjoying them here, a time to celebrate the peace and freedom of salvation in Christ by resting in Him today.

On Sabbath, we always have a special lunch, eaten on the good china. Unlike other meals that my wife cooks the same day we eat them, Sabbath lunch is prepared before, usually on Friday afternoon, so it is ready to be devoured on Sabbath. We are generally careful in what we eat and especially in what we feed our children, which means (with the occasional exception of fig or oatmeal cookies) that not many desserts are eaten at our table. But on Sabbath, there's always a dessert, always something tastier, richer, sweeter than any other day. This is a small thing, but it is the sum of the small things that makes the Sabbath a delight.

On Sabbath, when the children are napping, my wife and I share time together in a way that we rarely can the rest of the week. Sometimes we nap too, although we also read our Bibles and pray together. Morning and evening, we have family worship with the kids, but on these Sabbath afternoons, because I am not poised to rush off to work, and we both aren't exhausted at the end of the day, we have enjoyed many rich, spiritual moments together. Also, when so many marriages suffer from communication malfunction, often due simply to lack of time together, Sabbath allows us more time to listen and come close to each other. "The togetherness and closeness of body and soul that husbands and wives experience on the Sabbath," writes Samuele Bacchiocchi, "enable them to overcome any estrangement caused by the tension of the week passed and thus to experience a renewed sense of unity and commitment to God."[15] Who can place monetary value on moments like these?

The Lord has linked both the family and Sabbath. Marriage and Sabbath are two institutions specifically recorded in the Bible as coming directly from Eden. In the Decalogue, the Sabbath commandment is immediately followed by the order to honor our parents. These are the only two commandments that begin on a positive note. "Remember . . ." "Honor . . .," rather than "Thou shalt not . . ." Both commandments are related to God's call for holy living: " 'You shall be holy, for I the Lord your God am holy. Every one of you shall revere his mother and his father, and keep My Sabbaths' " (Leviticus 19:2, 3).

These links aren't coincidental. Sabbath is a "family commandment," because by this weekly polishing and tuning of our souls, we come closer to Jesus, who alone can keep our homes together. Jesus is preparing a place for us in heaven now, and He wants us there as families to be with His family (see Ephesians 3:15). The Sabbath is a divine way to prepare us.

" 'Wide is the gate and broad is the way that leads to destruction,' " Jesus warned, but " 'narrow is the gate and difficult is the way which leads to life' " (Matthew 7:13, 14). If so, then the Sabbath is a clear marker for the whole family, diverting them away from the broad path of destruction and leading them toward the narrow gate of eternal life while simultaneously making their trek through that gate a little more pleasant.

10

As the previous chapters have shown, I keep the Sabbath from sundown Friday to sundown Saturday, the biblical seventh day. Samuele Bacchiocchi, a recognized authority on the Sabbath, does the same.

Walter Chantry, quoted earlier, believes that Sunday is the Sabbath day for Christians, writing that "a first day Sabbath under the New Testament marks the promise and privilege of mankind entering God's rest with him and the possibility of doing so as a sinner through the finished redemptive work of Jesus Christ."[16] Most of the other Christians I have quoted, such as Norman Vincent Peale, keep Sunday. James Wesberry writes that the essence of the Lord's Day Alliance philosophy is stated as "the Divine authority and universal and perpetual obligation of the Sabbath, as manifested in the order and constitution of nature, declared in the revealed will of God, formulated in the Fourth Commandment of the Moral law, interpreted and applied by our Lord and Savior Jesus Christ, transferred to the Christian Sabbath, or Lord's Day, by Christ and His apostles, and approved by its beneficent influence upon personal and national life."[17]

Meanwhile Marva Dawn, though keeping Sunday, doesn't believe the day matters. "I will not enter into the debate," she says in her Sabbath book, "about whether the Sabbath should be observed on Saturday, the true seventh day of the Jewish custom, or on Sunday, set apart by the earliest Christians as the Lord's day. . . . The important thing is that a particular day is set aside as the Sabbath, and that it is faithfully observed every seven days so that God can imbue with a rhythm of six days of work and one day of ceasing work."[18]

Who's right?

On one level, Marva Dawn is. Those who take Sunday or Tuesday or Friday, any day, and keep it holy, will enjoy the blessing that comes from putting aside the secular and rejoicing for twenty-four hours in the freedom of salvation. A Sabbath kept properly will unquestionably enrich the life and Christian experience of the believer. On the level of merely seeking a blessing, any day will do.

On another level, however, her answer is lacking. God hasn't given us the option to pick which day we would choose to be our Sabbath, be it Monday or Saturday, any more than He made obedience to any of the other Ten Commandments optional. He gave a specific day. Most people believe that Sabbath is either Saturday or Sunday. It can't be both.

Who, which, is correct? Does God care which day, Saturday or Sunday, we choose? If He does, why? If not, why not?

PART THREE:

Remember the Sabbath

11

In the beginning there was Apsu, the sweet-water ocean; Tiamat, the saltwater ocean; and Mummu, their son. Apsu and Tiamat bore other gods, who, making too much noise, disturbed Apsu and Tiamat, who conspired to destroy them. A younger god, Ea, killed Apsu first. Tiamat, planning revenge, gave birth to eleven monsters, dragons, and serpents to battle for her, including "the great lion, the mad dog, and the scorpion-man." The younger gods knew that they couldn't defeat Tiamat, so, terrified, they appealed to Marduk, who agreed to fight for them—but only if they made him chief of all the gods. The others agreed: "To thee we have given totality of the whole universe."

Armed with a bow, a club, lightning, a net, eleven winds, and a storm chariot drawn by four frightful creatures "sharp of tooth, bearing poison," Marduk battled Tiamat. When Tiamat opened her mouth to devour Marduk, he drove in the wind until "the raging winds filled her belly." When she became distended, he shot an arrow into her mouth that tore her apart.

Marduk then used half her carcass to create the heavens; from the other half he formed the earth. He then mixed the blood of one of Tiamat's allies with the clay of the earth to make mankind, whose role was to do the work of the defeated gods.

Of course, not everyone in the ancient world accepted this Babylonian creation story. Many believed another Mesopotamian version of man's roots, in which the lesser gods, forced for forty years to dig canals on the earth's surface, unionized, formed a

43

picket line, and set fire to their tools. Deciding to appease the strikers, the major gods—mixing blood, clay, and spit—created man, who was made to finish digging the canals.

The Greeks, a bit more rational than most of their Near Eastern neighbors, saw creation mostly as the result of divine sexual activity. Gaea, the earth, came into existence on its own, while the trees, the sky, the seas, night, day, and hours were born of fornication. Even concepts such as justice, strife, and death were the offspring of carnal gods and goddesses. The god of sexual desire, Eros, was the primal force in creation.

In contrast to the fickle, violent, and carnal gods of the ancient pagan pantheon, the omniscient Creator depicted in Genesis purposely spoke the world into existence, not as the afterthought of a vicious battle between jealous, vengeful, and violent gods, but as a carefully planned and calculated act. God spoke, "and it was so."

In the pagan creation accounts, the gods had attributes of men—jealous, proud, passionate. In Genesis, man is given the attributes of God Himself: "In the image of God He created him; male and female He created them" (Genesis 1:27).

Unlike the Mesopotamian myths, in which men were created to be slaves, Genesis teaches that man was made to rule and to "have dominion over the fish of the sea, over the birds of the air, and over every living thing that moves on the earth" (verse 28).

In the pagan accounts, the world and those in it were flawed, as were the gods who made them. In Genesis, everyone and everything the Lord created came out perfect, even as He was perfect. God didn't stutter when He spoke the world into existence. "Then God saw everything that He had made, and indeed it was very good" (verse 31).

And though the Greek and Babylonian creation accounts have been relegated to fairy tales, Genesis remains, stubborn as roots. Despite attempts to destroy it with fire and sword or to dilute it with science and philosophy, the biblical creation record still burns in the souls of millions with the same authenticity as when Moses, sheep at his feet, penned it under the ancient sun. This account still commands such authority that people have gone to the highest court of the most powerful nation in history to stop it (not the Greek or Babylonian versions) from being taught in public schools. After 3,500 years, this is tenacity!

And no wonder, for the roots of humanity were not nourished in the polytheism of the pagans, but in the fertile soil of Genesis.

12

In every religion, men revere something—shrines, cities, even people. They kiss holy land; their ears clutch the syllables of holy men; they immerse themselves in holy water. Tangibles, touchables, holy things that they can see, revere, feel.

In Genesis, however, the first thing declared holy is not a hill, a shrine, or a place, but a block of time, the seventh day. "Then God blessed the seventh day and sanctified it" (Genesis 2:3). The word *sanctified* is translated from the Hebrew *qadosh*, which means "to set apart for holy use." Though Creation dealt with the heavens, the earth, the birds, the sea, and the beasts of the earth, all things of space—it was time, not space, that God first pronounced blessed and holy. This action makes sense, because, besides space, time is the dimension in which God's creation— the heavens, the earth, the birds, the sea, and the beasts of the earth—exist.

Also, if God had made one specific place holy, a hill, a spring, a city, not all people would have easy access to it. They would have to travel to worship there. But time comes to us, instead of us going to it. Once a week, at a thousand miles per hour (the approximate speed at which the earth rotates on its axis), the Sabbath circles the globe. Arriving on one sundown, leaving on the next, the seventh day washes over the planet each week like a huge cleansing wave. We never have to seek it. The day always finds us.

Meanwhile, holy cities can be burned. Holy people can be killed. Holy shrines can be looted. But time is beyond the fire and knife. No man can touch, much less destroy, it. Therefore, by making a special time holy, God has made the Sabbath invincible, placing it in an element that transcends any devices of mankind. Armies can sack cities, rulers can ban pilgrimages, but no military tank, no swirl of ink, can keep away the seventh day. We can no more stop the Sabbath than we can the sunrise. God protected His memorial to the objects of space, which are vulnerable to men, by placing it in time, which is not.

Finally, men can avoid holy things. They can hide from objects, people, places. But they can't flee from time. We can ignore it, be ignorant of it, hate it, but the Sabbath always comes, and nothing, no one, can stop it.

Skipping over no man, yet beyond the destructive grasp of all, the Sabbath stands as the universal, yet invincible, memorial of God's work in making mankind. Framed in time—the most basic element of God's creation—the Sabbath, more than any other biblical symbol, points us to the essence of our existence: that we are the handiwork of God. Thus, as the prime symbol of our roots, the Sabbath tells us also who we are, why we are, and where we are going, all in a mere twenty-four hours.

13

Week after week, year after year, millennium after millennium, the Sabbath, with the precision of the stars, settles over the earth every seventh sundown, drawing in its wake the Sabbath sun every seventh dawn. Because it memorializes Creation, the Sabbath is the first biblical symbol pointing to Jesus Christ, the Creator.

Talking about Jesus, Paul wrote, "By Him all things were created that are in heaven and that are on earth, visible and invisible, whether thrones or dominions or principalities or powers. All things were created through Him and for Him" (Colossians 1:16).

Paul wrote, too, that "for us there is only one God, the Father, of whom are all things, and we for Him; and one Lord Jesus Christ, through whom are all things, and through whom we live" (1 Corinthians 8:6).

Said John: "In the beginning was the Word, and the Word was with God, and the Word was God. . . . All things were made through Him, and without Him nothing was made that was made" (John 1:1, 3).

The Sabbath, therefore, stands as the only symbol of Christ, the Creator, that comes from a sinless world. The sacrificial animals that symbolized Jesus as the Lamb of God came only after the fall of mankind and the entrance of sin. The Sabbath predates sin, pointing to Jesus as the Creator of a perfect world.

After the Fall, God placed within the Sabbath, the symbol of a perfect creation, another aspect of His work. By pointing to

Creation, Sabbath points also to redemption, which is the restoration of that Creation. Redemption is to return us to the state that we enjoyed before sin entered, and this return can happen only through Jesus. "Being justified freely by His grace through the redemption that is in Christ Jesus" (Romans 3:24).

Creation and redemption are linked. Heaven and earth, created perfect by God, have been polluted by sin. Through the creative activity of Jesus Christ, however, they will be made over: "I saw a new heaven and a new earth, for the first heaven and the first earth had passed away" (Revelation 21:1); and through the redemptive activity of Jesus Christ, we will live in this new world: "We, according to His promise, look for new heavens and a new earth in which righteousness dwells" (2 Peter 3:13).

For centuries, the Jews have seen in the Sabbath a symbol of Messianic redemption. One legend states that if the Jews were obedient to the commandments of God, they would receive a reward in the Messianic era. Having asked to see an example of that era, they were told, "The Sabbath is an example of the world to come."[19] Another Jewish source calls the Sabbath "a reminder of the two worlds—this world and the world to come—it is an example of both. For the Sabbath is joy, holiness, and rest; joy is part of this world; holiness and rest are part of the world to come."[20] In modern times, Rabbi Abraham Joshua Heschel wrote that on the Sabbath, "man is touched by a moment of actual redemption; as if for a moment the spirit of the Messiah moved over the face of the earth."[21]

Of course, not only the spirit of the Messiah moved over the earth, but the Messiah Himself. Nevertheless, the Jews correctly saw in the Sabbath a sign of Messianic redemption, a sign that many Christians have acknowledged as well. According to scholar Samuele Bacchiocchi, "the Sabbath has been used by God both in the Old Testament and the New Testament to give His people the assurance and experience of a present and future divine redemption." German theologian Karl Barth's view of the Sabbath, summarized by James Brown, is that "the fundamental meaning of the Sabbath is thus that it is a sign of salvation altogether, first and last, of God, in His covenant relation with His creature."[22]

Thus the Sabbath, symbol of creation and redemption, refers to Jesus, the Creator and Redeemer. The animal sacrifices symbolized Jesus as Redeemer, not Creator; the Sabbath came to symbolize both. The Sabbath, therefore, remains the most complete insignia of Jesus Christ, a sign of the sinless world He first created, and of the sinless world He will create again for those redeemed through His blood.

14

The seventh-day Sabbath, Saturday, is often denigrated as the "old Jewish Sabbath." That view has problems, however, because the seventh-day Sabbath, in its origin, purpose, and meaning, had nothing to do with Jews. The Sabbath is associated with Jews only because they have been keeping it for millennia, but that still doesn't make it Jewish.

New Yorkers have been observing Christmas for years. Is, therefore, Christmas exclusively a New York holiday? Christmas predates New Yorkers, wasn't invented by New Yorkers, didn't start with New Yorkers, wasn't made specifically for New Yorkers, and is kept by others besides New Yorkers.

The same with the Sabbath. It predates Jews, wasn't invented by Jews, didn't start with Jews, wasn't made specifically for Jews, and is kept by others besides Jews. Sabbath, therefore, no more belongs exclusively to Jews than Christmas does to the Big Apple.

Many Christians insist that the seventh-day Sabbath is for the Jews only. "The biblical view is unequivocal," writes theologian Harold Dressler. "The Sabbath originated in Israel as God's special institution for His people."[23]

The Bible is unequivocal about the origin of the Sabbath, and it had nothing to do with Jews. God blessed and sanctified the seventh day at the end of the Creation week, thousands of years before the Hebrew nation existed. The word *Hebrew* doesn't even appear in the Bible until Genesis 14:13, in reference to Abram (Abraham), who didn't appear until many centuries after

Creation. The first Jews, technically speaking, were the children of Judah—Abraham's great grandson. The Bible doesn't even mention *Jews* until 2 Kings 16:6 (KJV), long after the Creation account. The Jews didn't invent Sabbath; on the contrary, it was already there, waiting to be kept holy by the followers of the Lord, who in antiquity were mostly Jews.

In Genesis 2:1-3—still in Creation week—the Bible says:

> Thus the heavens and the earth, and all the host of them, were finished. And on the seventh day God ended His work which He had done, and He rested on the seventh day from all His work which He had done. Then God blessed the seventh day and sanctified it, because in it He rested from all His work which God had created and made.

The fourth commandment at Mount Sinai reads:

> Remember the Sabbath day, to keep it holy. Six days you shall labor and do all your work, but the seventh day is the Sabbath of the Lord your God. In it you shall do no work: you, nor your son, nor your daughter, nor your manservant, nor your maidservant, nor your cattle, nor your stranger who is within your gates. For in six days the Lord made the heavens and the earth, the sea, and all that is in them, and rested the seventh day. Therefore the Lord blessed the Sabbath day and hallowed it (Exodus 20:8-11).

The fourth commandment in Exodus obviously points back to the Creation Sabbath. The Hebrew words used in Exodus 20:11 to say that God *blessed* and *hallowed* (or *sanctified*) the seventh day are from the same root words used in Genesis 2 to say that God *blessed* and *sanctified* the seventh day. Both places use the Hebrew phrase *yom hassbi'i* for "the seventh day" (Genesis 2:2; Exodus 20:11). Both use the same word for *made*, *'sh* (see Genesis 2:2, KJV; Exodus 20:11), to describe God's creative activity. Also, the noun *Sabbath* (*Shabbat* in Hebrew) used in

Exodus comes from the same root, *shbt* ("to cease from labor"), used in Genesis to explain that God "rested" (*shbt*) on the seventh day. Clearly, the fourth commandment refers to the Creation Sabbath.

Jesus said, "The Sabbath was made for man" (Mark 2:27); that first Sabbath, therefore, had been made for man too. At Creation, mankind consisted only of Adam and Eve, so they must have kept the Sabbath. Otherwise, if it was only for the Jews, why would the Lord have blessed the seventh day and sanctified the Sabbath so many centuries prior to the Jewish nation?

By its nature as a memorial to the creation of mankind and the world, the Sabbath is universal. Framed in a block of time that comes to everyone everywhere, the Sabbath is boundless, transcendent, and purposely not confined to one land or geographic area. It reaches all people each week because it is for all people. Everyone should keep the Sabbath because everyone, white, black, Indian—not just Jews—was created by God, and the Sabbath stands as the timeless, universal, and indestructible memorial of that creation. Why would a symbol of all creation be limited to one people alone, when all were the Lord's handiwork?

Many Jews understand the universality of the Sabbath. Jewish philosopher Martin Buber writes that because it "is rooted in the very beginnings of the world itself," the Sabbath "is the common property of all, and all ought to enjoy it without restriction."[24]

"But after the whole world had been completed according to the perfect nature of the number six," wrote Philo Judaeus, first-century Jewish scholar, "the Father hallowed the day following, the seventh, praising it and calling it holy. For that day is a festival, not of one city or country, but of all the earth; a day which alone it is right to call the day of festival for all people, and the birthday of the world."

Many Christians understand this truth as well. "The Sabbath was not for Israel merely, but for the world," wrote Adventist pioneer Ellen White. "It had been made known to man in Eden, and, like the other precepts of the Decalogue, it is of imperishable obligation. Of that law of which the fourth commandment forms a part, Christ declares, 'Till heaven and earth pass, one jot or one tittle shall in no wise pass from the law.' So long as the heavens and the earth endure, the Sabbath will continue as a sign of the Creator's power. And when Eden shall bloom on earth again, God's holy rest day will be honored by all beneath the sun. 'From one Sabbath to another' the inhabitants of the glorified new earth shall go up 'to worship before Me, saith the Lord.' Matt. 5:18; Isa. 66:23."[25]

Of course, the Jews have kept Sabbath longer than anyone else, which is why it is commonly linked to them. People keeping anything for more than 3,500 years would have some insights on what it means. But to claim that the Sabbath is exclusively Jewish—when it was introduced before Jews existed, when it wasn't created specifically for Jews, and when it has been kept by others besides the Jews—is to miss the purpose and meaning of the Sabbath as a memorial to the creation of all mankind, not just Hebrews.

The "old Jewish Sabbath"?

It might be old, but it is not so Jewish.

15

Nevertheless, many sincere Christians believe that prior to the law at Mount Sinai, Sabbath keeping was not an obligatory commandment and was not observed. The Bible, however, proves that prior to Sinai, the Sabbath *was* an obligatory commandment and *was* observed.

Exodus 16, dealing with the journeys of the Jews after the escape from Pharaoh's chariots, opens "on the fifteenth day of the second month after they departed from the land of Egypt" (verse 1). Sinai doesn't come until at least two weeks later, "in the third month after the children of Israel had gone out of the land of Egypt" (Exodus 19:1).

In the account of Exodus 16, because the people were hungry, the Lord promised to " 'rain bread [manna] from heaven for you.' " He said also that He would " 'test them, whether they will walk in My Law or not' " (Exodus 16:4).

What law? In all biblical history, the giving of the law is not yet mentioned. The Jews, however, must have known the law, or how could God test them on it?

" 'And the people shall go out and gather a certain quota every day, that I may test them. . . . And it shall be on the sixth day that they shall prepare what they bring in, and it shall be twice as much as they gather daily' " (Exodus 16:4, 5).

Why gather twice as much on the sixth day?

"Then Moses said, 'Eat that today, for today is a Sabbath to the Lord; today you will not find it in the field. Six days you shall gather it, but on the seventh day, which is the Sabbath, there will be none' '' (verses 25, 26).

Some Israelites, however, went out on the Sabbath to gather manna anyway, an act for which they were rebuked. "And the Lord said to Moses, 'How long do you refuse to keep My commandments and My laws? See! For the Lord has given you the Sabbath; therefore He gives you on the sixth day bread for two days. Let every man remain in his place; let no man go out of his place on the seventh day.' So the people rested on the seventh day" (verses 28-30).

The Lord's rebuke, "*How long* do you refuse to keep My commandments and My laws?" shows that their disobedience was not a new phenomenon. The question of "How long?" implies that law breaking had been an ongoing problem. The Israelites must have already known the law; otherwise, why would God have chastised them for continually transgressing it?

Verse 29 reads, "The Lord has given you the Sabbath." The Hebrew word for *has given*, *ntn*, is vocalized in the past tense in contrast to the same word for *gives*, *ntn*, in the same verse, vocalized to read, "He gives you on the sixth day bread." Obviously, the Sabbath had been given to the Jews even before this incident, which was weeks before Mount Sinai. It's clear, beyond dispute, that the Sabbath existed before Sinai and that the Jews knew about it prior to the law at Sinai too.

According to scholar Gerhard Hasel, Exodus 16 "reveals that the Sabbath institution was known before the giving of the law on Mount Sinai and before its appearance in the wilderness of sin."[26]

Jewish theologian Martin Buber agrees, writing that the Sabbath "is not introduced for the first time even in the wilderness of Sin, where the manna is found. Here, too, it is proclaimed as something which is already in existence."[27]

Martin Luther recognized that the Sabbath existed prior to Sinai: "Hence you can see that the Sabbath was before the law of Moses came, and has existed from the beginning of the world. Especially have the devout, who have preserved the true faith, met together and called upon God on this day."[28]

The "people rested on the seventh day" (verse 30). No one ordered them to rest; they were told merely not to gather manna, to bake it, or to leave their "place." The verb for *rested* used in Exodus 16 is from *shbt*, found in Genesis 2:3, when God "rested" on the seventh day. After that first Sabbath, this verb is not used in reference to Sabbath keeping again (Sabbath keeping isn't mentioned again) until it appears in this incident. Somehow the Israelites knew they were to "rest" (*shbt*) anyway, and the only way could be from the Creation Sabbath.

Because manna had never fallen before, Exodus 16 records specific instructions for its use on the Sabbath, a situation that the Israelites had never faced before.

In this same incident, the Lord decided to "test" His chosen people as to " 'whether they will walk in My law or not' " (verse 4). The Sabbath was the test. When they disobeyed, God's rebuke was " 'How long do you refuse to keep My commandments and My laws?' " (verse 28). Obedience to the Sabbath symbolized obedience to *all* His laws.

This principle appears in the New Testament: "Whoever shall keep the whole law, and yet stumble in one point, he is guilty of all. For He who said, 'Do not commit adultery,' also said, 'Do not murder.' Now if you do not commit adultery, but you do murder, you have become a transgressor of the law" (James 2:10, 11). According to Exodus 16, if you transgress the Sabbath commandment, then you become "guilty of all" as well.

The first test regarding God's law for His chosen nation after their escape from Egypt was the Sabbath. This makes sense, because of all the commandments, the Sabbath mostly clearly points to Jesus Christ as Creator and Redeemer. Jesus Himself led the children of Israel through their wilderness experiences and thus was the One who tested them regarding His law.

"Moreover, brethren," wrote the apostle Paul, "I do not want you to be unaware that all our fathers were under the cloud, all passed through the sea, all were baptized into Moses in the cloud and in the sea, all ate the same spiritual food, and all drank the same spiritual drink. For they drank of that spiritual Rock that followed them, and that Rock was Christ" (1 Corinthians 10:1-4). Christ has said, " 'If you love Me, keep My commandments' " (John 14:15). For ancient Israel, a test of that love was the Sabbath commandment.

16

If the Jews knew about God's law, including the Sabbath, before Sinai, where did they learn about it? The answer, like a fine thread, weaves through the Old and New Testaments, helping stitch them into one.

When the Lord first appeared to Moses, promising deliverance for the worn, brick-broken children of Israel, He said, " 'Thus you shall say to the children of Israel: "The Lord God of your fathers, the God of Abraham, the God of Isaac, and the God of Jacob, has sent me to you. This is My name forever, and this is My memorial to all generations" ' " (Exodus 3:15).

From Creation in Genesis to Sinai in Exodus, it was always this same God, the God of the fathers, *Adonai Elohim*, "the same yesterday, today, and forever" (Hebrews 13:8), whom the faithful worshiped. The patriarchal episodes in Genesis recount the history of the followers of this God, those who obeyed Him amid a world immersed in paganism, idolatry, and false religion. Whether describing Noah, whom the Lord found "righteous" before Him (see Genesis 7:1), or Abraham, whose belief was "accounted to him for righteousness" (Galatians 3:6), the Bible preserved the stories of the patriarchs' worship of the Lord.

Included in this worship was obedience to His commandments. The Lord said that He would multiply Jacob's descendants because his grandfather Abraham "obeyed My voice and kept My charge, My commandments, My statutes, and My laws" (Genesis 26:5). What statutes, commandments, and laws? The giving of these commandments, statues, and laws is never mentioned in Genesis, and yet because of Abraham's obedience to them, the Lord promised to bless Jacob's seed.

Prior to the thunderings and lightning at Sinai, the law must have been known. Otherwise, during this period—about 2,000 years—did no standard of right and wrong exist? For all those years (equal to the span of the entire Christian dispensation so far), did God allow men and women to do as they pleased, with no divine warning against evil? How could the Sodomites or those who perished in the Flood be condemned if no law against their acts existed? The Bible says that "sin is the transgression of the law" (1 John 3:4, KJV); thus, if there were no law, there could be no sin.

In the story of Cain and Abel, the Lord said to Cain: " 'If you do well, will you not be accepted? And if you do not do well, sin lies at the door' " (Genesis 4:7). Of course, if Cain had not been aware of God's law, he could not have known about sin because, as Paul wrote, "by the law is the knowledge of sin" (Romans 3:20).

When Joseph was tempted by his Egyptian master's wife, he cried out, " 'How then can I do this great wickedness, and sin against God?' " (Genesis 39:9). How could Joseph have known that adultery was a "sin against God" unless he knew of God's law concerning it? "I would not have known sin," says Paul, "except through the law" (Romans 7:7). Was it any different for Joseph?

Before the destruction of Sodom and Gomorrah, the Lord said to Abraham, " 'Because the outcry against Sodom and Gomorrah is great, and because their sin is very grievous . . .' " (Genesis 18:20). What sin? The Bible says that "sin is not imputed [charged] when there is no law" (Romans 5:13).

Writing about Lot in Sodom and Gomorrah, Peter said that this "righteous man, dwelling among them, tormented his righteous soul from day to day by seeing and hearing their lawless deeds" (2 Peter 2:8). Their deeds couldn't have been lawless unless there was a law against those deeds, any more than it could be unlawful for a person to sleep in green socks unless a law forbids it.

If in America a law has to exist before one is punished for

breaking it, would God do any less? If no law existed, God would not have punished transgression, because "where there is no law there is no transgression" (Romans 4:15).

What type of God would wipe out the world with a flood, or Sodom and Gomorrah with fire, unless those people had known that they were sinning? And because, according to the Bible, only through the law is the knowledge of sin, the law must have been revealed prior to Sinai.

17

If God's law existed during the thousands of years before Sinai, why didn't He spell it out in Genesis, as He did in Exodus?

First, Genesis is not a book about law, but a brief survey of origins and a history of the worship of the Lord from Eden to Egypt. It recounts the line of God's faithful followers, a small group that eventually narrowed down to a single family, who over many generations worshiped the Creator amid universal apostasy.

Second, Genesis covers about two thousand years of history in only fifty short chapters, about forty years per division. Such short space doesn't leave room for details. Genesis, for example, says nothing about the future reward of the righteous. Did not God's people in Genesis rejoice in the hope and promise that the Lord offered? The book of Hebrews, talking about the patriarchs, says: "These all died in faith, not having received the promises, but having seen them afar off were assured of them, embraced them, and confessed that they were strangers and pilgrims on the earth." It said, too, that these ancient people "desire[d] a better, that is, a heavenly country" (Hebrews 11:13, 16). What promises? What heavenly country? None of these are specified in Genesis, yet the patriarchs embraced them anyway.

Hebrews says that Abraham prepared to offer up Isaac, knowing that "God was able to raise him up, even from the dead" (Hebrews 11:19). Abraham knew of the resurrection of the dead, but where did he learn of it? That doctrine is not recorded anywhere in Genesis.

Third, God's law might have been so universally known, especially by His followers, that no need existed for the Holy Spirit to inspire Moses to write about it in Genesis. The way the law suddenly appears in Exodus 16—" 'How long do you refuse to keep My commandments and My laws?' " (verse 28)—without any explanation of what that law was or where it came from proves that it already was understood.

Somehow, although Genesis doesn't say how, God's law had been revealed and taught in the ancient world long before the giving of the Ten Commandments at Mount Sinai. When God established Israel as the covenant people, He didn't ask them to promulgate something new, something that had never been heard of before. Instead, as their fathers before them—Noah, Abraham, Isaac, and Jacob—they were entrusted with preserving the worship and knowledge of God, which had been overwhelmed by paganism, idolatry, and false religion. Included in that knowledge was His law. And included in that law, even at its center, was the Sabbath.

18

During the entire patriarchal period, however, no direct command to keep holy the seventh day is recorded. Neither can we find a direct command against stealing, murdering, committing adultery, or idolatry. From the book of Deuteronomy to 2 Kings—a span covering the wilderness journeying; the capture of Canaan; the era of the judges; the reigns of Saul, David, and Solomon; the division of the Jewish kingdom; and beyond— no mention is made of Sabbath keeping, though during all that time it was enforced with the death penalty. From Joshua to Nehemiah (almost a thousand years), the Feast of Booths, though never mentioned, was certainly kept as well.

Silence therefore proves nothing, except that these commands were probably taken for granted.

The patriarchs apparently knew about the seven-day "week." Numerous times in Genesis, a seven-day period is depicted (see Genesis 7:4, 10; 8:10, 12); meanwhile, Jacob's nuptial activities are, technically, described as a week. "Fulfill her week, and we will give you this one also for the service which you will serve with me still another seven years" (Genesis 29:27). The incident with the manna in Exodus 16—" 'Six days you shall gather it, but on the seventh day, which is the Sabbath, there will be none' " (verse 26)—proves that the seven-day week was known and that it climaxed on Sabbath. Certainly all the patriarchs— worshipers of the God of the Fathers (they were the Fathers!)— kept the weekly Sabbath as did the Jews, who worshiped the same God.

Unlike any of the other Ten Commandments, such as the prohibitions against adultery, murder, and theft, the Sabbath is the only one, before Sinai, specifically referred to as a commandment. After the Israelites transgressed the holy day, the Lord asked, " 'How long do you refuse to keep My commandments?' " (verse 28). Thus the Sabbath was the only part of the Decalogue called a "commandment" up to that point.

Also, the period between the end of Creation week and Sinai was demarcated by references to rest on the seventh-day Sabbath. In Genesis 2, creation ended when God Himself "rested" (*shbt*) on the seventh day, while in Exodus 16, just prior to Sinai, the people rested (*shbt*) on the seventh day as well. God set the example at Creation; the Jews followed it in the desert. By its nature as a symbol of Creation, the Sabbath surely had been observed by those faithful to the Creator. Established at Creation to commemorate that event, was the Sabbath put on hold for two thousand years only to appear suddenly, without warning, in Exodus, to get the Jews in trouble for not keeping it? Did not the Lord for all those centuries have a symbol of His creative and also His redemptive work? Didn't those people have the blessings of a weekly day of rest?

For the next two thousand years, His chosen nation, the Jews, kept the Sabbath; for the next two thousand, Christians have, however lazily, kept (or at least acknowledged) a Sabbath. What about the first two thousand years of earth? Did not God have His holy day then as well?

19

Imagine Mount Sinai, an inferno of flames and smoke, "because the Lord descended upon it in fire" (Exodus 19:18) while lightning exploded as if the sky cracked and heaven's glory flashed through. Trembling, the children of Israel huddled as God hewed the Ten Commandments into their souls.

" 'You speak with us,' " they later begged Moses, " 'and we will hear; but let not God speak with us, lest we die' " (Exodus 20:19).

If, however, the Israelites already knew of God's law, including the Sabbath, why the big production at Sinai?

Numerous times the Lord had promised the Fathers that He would make of them a great and populous people, as if each seed in their loins would bear fruit that would blossom into the nation with whom He would establish His everlasting covenant (see Genesis 17:19). This promise He fulfilled with the children of Israel at Sinai. Nevertheless, this people had just spent four centuries immersed in one of the most polytheistic and idolatrous cultures in the ancient Near East. Few environments could have been more alien and polluting to the faith of the Fathers than the Egypt of the pharaohs. If, in one generation, American TV can go from censoring Elvis's jiggling hips to allowing Madonna to parade around in nothing but a black teddy—imagine what four centuries among the idols, pyramids, and gods of Egypt did to the Jews!

No sooner had God's voice from Sinai stopped echoing in their ears than they made and worshiped a golden calf! This animal was commonly revered in Egypt as a god, which explained why—despite the commandment that warned against making and worshiping an idol (see Exodus 20:4)—the Israelites chanted, " 'This is your god, O Israel, that brought you out of the land of Egypt!' " (Exodus 32:4)! If still so influenced by their former environment that they would lapse into idolatry just after such a powerful manifestation of God at Sinai, what would have happened if, instead of thundering down His law to Israel, the Lord had meekly suggested that, perhaps, they might want to obey His Ten Recommendations?

For all the display associated with giving the Ten Commandments at Sinai, they weren't first introduced here. The law had previously existed; at Sinai, it was formalized into the covenant between God and Israel. " 'He declared to you His covenant,' " Moses said, " 'which He commanded you to perform, that is, the Ten Commandments; and He wrote them on two tablets of stone' " (Deuteronomy 4:13). At Sinai the law was institutionalized into their faith, and they were to obey it as their end of the bargain.

Unfortunately, as the golden calf debacle proved (see Exodus 32), the law brings only death, which is why the Lord established the sanctuary service soon after He formalized the Ten Commandments. This elaborate system, based on animal sacrifices, pointed the sinner to his only hope of salvation, the Messiah, who would be his sacrifice (typified in the death of the animals) and his intercessor (typified in the Levitical priesthood). Because "it is not possible that the blood of bulls and goats could take away sins" (Hebrews 10:4), Jesus Himself gave His life, the true " 'Lamb of God who takes away the sin of the world' " (John 1:29). In the old and the new covenants, God's law points out sin. "I would not have known sin," wrote Paul, "except through the law" (Romans 7:7). Sin, in turn, can be forgiven only by the blood of Christ.

Thus, at Sinai, the Ten Commandments were reiterated to Israel as part of God's covenant with them, and in the midst of those commandments was the seventh-day Sabbath, singled out as a sign between the Lord and His people. " 'Therefore the children of Israel shall keep the Sabbath, to observe the Sabbath throughout their generations as a perpetual covenant. It is a sign between Me and the children of Israel forever; for in six days the Lord made the heavens and the earth, and on the seventh day He rested and was refreshed' '' (Exodus 31:16, 17).

Here, too, the Sabbath's origin is linked, not to Sinai, but to Creation, long before Israel. Keeping the Sabbath didn't make Israel God's chosen people; rather, because they *were* God's chosen people, they kept Sabbath as a sign that—unlike the nations around them—they worshiped the true God, the One who created the heavens and the earth in six days. Sabbath didn't begin at Sinai for the Jews; it had been there from the world's birth, a sign that the Lord was Creator. Because Israel worshiped the Creator, they kept His Sabbath.

20

Besides the seventh-day Sabbath, other sabbath days were given to the Hebrew nation as part of such annual feasts as Passover, Pentecost, and the Feast of Tabernacles (see Leviticus 23). Unlike the weekly Sabbath that memorialized Creation, these other sabbaths were distinctly Israelite—often tied to their presence in the Holy Land—and were purposely distinguished from the seventh-day "Sabbaths of the Lord" (verse 38). How?

First, God Himself made the distinction. After delineating to the Hebrews the festivals, convocations, new moons, and sabbaths that they were to observe, He said: " 'These are the feasts of the Lord which you shall proclaim to be holy convocations . . . *besides the Sabbaths of the Lord*' " (Leviticus 23:37, 38, emphasis supplied). What were these "Sabbaths of the Lord"? Exodus says that the weekly seventh day " 'is the Sabbath of the Lord your God' " (Exodus 20:10). Thus, the Lord Himself differentiated between the seventh-day Sabbath, "the Sabbaths of the Lord," which were tied to Creation, and the ceremonial sabbaths, which were tied to the sacrificial system of feasts, convocations, and new moons.

The seventh-day Sabbath, instituted at the end of Creation week, existed prior both to the Jews and to Sinai; the other sabbaths, not given until Sinai, didn't exist prior to the Hebrew nation or Sinai. They were given specifically to the Jews, because they were specifically for the Jews.

The commandment regarding observance of the seventh-day Sabbath of the Lord was written by God Himself on imperishable tablets of stone and placed inside the ark of the covenant (see Deuteronomy 10:2-5); the commandments regarding the other sabbaths were written by Moses on perishable parchment placed outside the ark, separate and distinct from the Ten Commandments.

Unquestionably, the greatest difference between the seventh-day "Sabbaths of the Lord" and the sabbaths of the Israelite feasts and sacrificial system is that the seventh-day Sabbath was not inaugurated as a shadow, a type, of Christ's ministry as were the other sabbaths, linked only to the annual feasts of the sacrificial system. Almost all Christians would agree that at the death of Jesus, when "the veil of the temple was torn in two from top to bottom" (Matthew 27:51), the sacrificial system of ancient Israel, which included the festivals, new moons, and ceremonial sabbaths, was terminated. They had all met their fulfillment in Christ.

The seventh-day Sabbath, however, did not serve the same ceremonial purpose as these other sabbath days. "The Decalogue's fourth commandment," wrote Walter Chantry, "does not point forward to Christ with shadowy images of him. It clearly points back to creation and to God's rest."[29]

The seventh-day Sabbath could not have been a shadow of Christ's death because, like marriage—and unlike the sacrificial system—it was instituted before sin, before Christ needed to die. It wasn't created originally to point to the cross. The seventh-day Sabbath was not fulfilled at the cross any more than was marriage, which is symbolic of Christ's relationship with the church (see Matthew 25:1-12; Revelation 19:7, 9). Instead, the seventh-day Sabbath, instituted in Eden as an everlasting memorial of Christ's creatorship, remains distinct from the temporary system of sacrifices, new moons, and sabbaths tied to the Hebrew sanctuary service, all of which served as shadows of Christ's death and His high priestly ministry (see Hebrews, chapters 7-9).

21

From the establishment of the covenant at Mount Sinai until the dispersion of the Jews by the Romans in the first century A.D., the seventh-day Sabbath pulsed each week at the heart of the Israelite nation. Obedience to the Sabbath was a test of Israel's fidelity to all the commandments—as the incident with the manna proved. They were warned against disobedience to the Sabbath command: " 'If you will not heed Me to hallow the Sabbath day,' " they were told, " 'such as not carrying a burden when entering the gates of Jerusalem on the Sabbath day, then I will kindle a fire in its gates, and it shall devour the palaces of Jerusalem, and it shall not be quenched' " (Jeremiah 17:27).

On the other hand, the Lord promised that if the Jews would " 'bring no burden through the gates of this city on the Sabbath day, but hallow the Sabbath day, to do no work in it' " (Jeremiah 17:24), then He would bring upon them all the great blessings that He had promised if they would obey (see verses 25, 26; Deuteronomy 28).

Both thematically and geometrically, the Sabbath forms the hub of the Ten Commandments. It consists of fifty-five *Hebrew* words and sits between the sixty-seven Hebrew words of the first three commandments and the forty-one Hebrew words of the last six. "Thus," writes Old Testament scholar Jacques Doukhan, "it contains about half as many words as the rest of the Decalogue (108) and is placed in the middle of it."[30]

Placed in the heart of the Ten Commandments between the first three, which deal with man's relationship to God (" 'You shall love the Lord your God with all your heart, with all your soul, and with all your mind' ''), and the last six, which deal with man's relationship to man ('' 'You shall love your neighbor as yourself' '' [Matthew 22:37, 39])—the Sabbath functions as a bridge between Christ's two great commands. "The Sabbath," writes Roy Branson, "is the arch holding together the structure of the law. Coming as it does between the outline of commitment to God and obligations to fellow men, the Sabbath commandment is the hinge of the two tablets of stone."[31] It links, in a sense, heaven and earth.

Meanwhile, the fourth commandment alone explains why we should obey the other nine. We shouldn't have any other gods before the Lord because, as the Sabbath commandment says, He is the Creator. We shouldn't make or worship idols because God alone, as the One who made us, deserves our worship. We shouldn't use the Lord's name in vain because as Creator, He deserves respect. Thus, none of the first three commandments, which deal with the vertical dimension between man and God, quite make sense unless understood in relationship to the fourth.

The other six commandments, honoring our parents, not stealing, not committing adultery, etc., focus on a horizontal, person-to-person plane. Because we all are made by the God depicted in the fourth commandment, we are obliged to treat each other with the deference that we deserve, formed as we are in the image of that Creator. If we were the result of an amoral accident, mere flukes of "slime and time" alone—then what absolute moral imperative would bind us to treat each other with respect? None, which is why the implications of the fourth commandment make obedience to the last six so important.

Thus the Sabbath played an important part in the faith of God's Old Testament people, even, some would argue, the most important part. "One can say without exaggeration," wrote Jewish essayist Ahad Ha-'Am, "that more than Israel kept the Sabbath, the Sabbath has kept Israel."[32]

Now, however, comes the rub: all Christians, even the most aggressive anti-Sabbatarians, agree that the Jews were to keep the seventh-day Sabbath. But what about Christians today? What role, if any, does the Sabbath have for *new* covenant believers, those who follow the *New* Testament teaching of salvation by grace, not by the works of the law? What, if any, are their Sabbath obligations?

PART FOUR:

The Sabbath Was Made for Man

22

On a windy Saturday afternoon, a widow was raking crisp leaves, when her neighbor, a Seventh-day Adventist, leaned over the white wooden fence that separated their lawns.

"Don't you know," the Adventist said without a hello, "that you shouldn't be working? Today is God's Sabbath."

Stopping, the widow looked up, her eyes momentarily blurring in thought. Then focusing on her neighbor, she smiled and said, "But Jesus healed on the Sabbath."

"Well," he huffed, "two wrongs don't make a right!"

This story, told by a popular evangelical, expresses a common perception. Seventh-day Adventists can seem more preoccupied with the Sabbath than with Jesus. Seventh-day Adventists often appear to have made the Sabbath, not Jesus, their Saviour. And Seventh-day Adventists sometimes act as if salvation hinges on Sabbath keeping alone.

The Sabbath is supposed to reveal Jesus, not eclipse Him. If that truth has slipped away from some Adventists, they are not alone. On a Sabbath in ancient Israel, Jesus healed a beggar boy blind from birth. " 'Since the world began,' " exclaimed the one whose eyes now filled with light, " 'it has been unheard of that anyone opened the eyes of one who was born blind' " (John 9:32).

The Pharisees had other concerns.

" 'This Man is not from God,' " they insisted, " 'because He does not keep the Sabbath' " (verse 16). So preoccupied with the sanctity of the seventh day that they missed the One who sanctified it!

About one hundred thousand Sabbaths later, some Adventists—when they meet other Christians—don't ask, "What has Jesus done in your life?" or "Isn't it wonderful what Jesus has done for us?" Instead, they immediately ask, "Why don't you keep the Sabbath?" How many Christians have rejected the Sabbath because of Seventh-day Adventists who seem to make the day, not Jesus Christ, their Saviour?

The Sabbath is important, but not more important than Christ. Without Jesus, the Sabbath is merely one day in seven. Without Jesus, one can't keep *any* day holy. Without Jesus, Sabbath keepers become like the Pharisees in the Gospel account or the man in the evangelical's anecdote.

But with Jesus . . . ?

That's another story.

23

From the first words of Genesis ("In the beginning" [1:1]), until almost the final words of Revelation ("Even so, come, Lord Jesus" [22:20]), the Bible tells of Jesus Christ. The first book deals with His creation of the world and the last with redemption at His second coming (two themes also found in the Sabbath). The rest of the Bible, between Genesis and Revelation, covers everything else about Jesus.

And nowhere is Christ better covered than in the Gospels, the remarkable story of how the Lord took humanity upon Himself and lived among human beings. "The Word became flesh and dwelt among us" (John 1:14).

As "the express image" of His Father's person (see Hebrews 1:3), Jesus came to reveal God to a world that had long lost sight of Him. When Philip asked to see the Father, Jesus replied, " 'Have I been with you so long, and yet you have not known Me, Philip? He who has seen Me has seen the Father' " (John 14:9). Jesus, "equal with God" (Philippians 2:6), is the greatest manifestation of God that the world has ever witnessed, and never was that manifestation better revealed than when He, the Lord Himself, hung upon a cross, taking our sins, which He didn't deserve, so that we might possess His glory and righteousness, which we didn't deserve (see 2 Corinthians 5:17-21).

Jesus is the source of all light, life, and power, the One in whom " 'we live and move and have our being' " (Acts 17:28), the One through whom "all things were created" and through whom "all things consist" (Colossians 1:16, 17). In contrast to great men throughout history who have spent their lives seeking truth, teaching truth, even claiming to possess truth—Jesus declared, " *'I am* . . . the truth' " (John 14:6, emphasis supplied). Jesus, the "true Light which gives light to every man who comes into the world" (John 1:9), is the source from which we should seek light and truth. He *is* light and truth.

Therefore, as we seek light on the truth of the Sabbath as it applies to Christians today, we must first seek Jesus. What did Jesus, when He was here with us in the flesh, say about the Sabbath? What was His command? What was His example?

Jesus called Himself "Lord of the Sabbath" (Mark 2:28), and thus from the Lord of the Sabbath, better than anyone else, we can learn what the Lord teaches about His Sabbath.

24

A few weeks after becoming a believer, I was confronted with the question of the seventh-day Sabbath. Looking for an escape, I asked an evangelical friend if I could ignore the Sabbath.

"Of course," Danny answered sincerely, "Jesus abolished the Ten Commandments."

Somehow, even as a newborn Christian, I wasn't convinced. It's not surprising why. A cursory look at what Jesus said regarding the Ten Commandments (the moral law) shows that far from diminishing or abolishing the commandments, Jesus amplified them.

If someone " 'is angry with his brother without a cause' " (Matthew 5:22), Jesus said, that person has essentially broken the commandment against murder. " 'Whoever,' " He said, " 'looks at a woman to lust for her has already committed adultery with her in his heart' " (verse 28). These verses hardly sound as if Jesus abolished the Ten Commandments. Rather, these words explain what He meant a few verses earlier when He proclaimed: " 'Do not think that I came to destroy the Law or the Prophets. I did not come to destroy but to *fulfill*' " (Matthew 5:17, emphasis supplied).

Some argue that Jesus has reduced the Ten Commandments to two: " ' "You shall love the Lord your God with all your heart, with all your soul, and with all your mind," ' " and " ' "You shall love your neighbor as yourself" ' " (Matthew 22:37, 39).

Did Jesus mean, therefore, that His followers can worship idols, have other gods before Him, and use His name in vain, just as long as they love God with all their hearts, souls, and minds? Did Jesus mean that Christians can steal from their neighbor, kill him, and commit adultery with his wife, just as long as they love Him as themselves? Of course not! By these two commands Christ simply *summarized* the two great principles of the ten: love to God (as expressed in the first four) and love to man (as expressed in the last six). The apostle John put it another way: "This is the love of God, that we keep His commandments" (1 John 5:3).

Jesus warned that many who think they are Christians will not enter the kingdom of heaven because they haven't done the will of His Father. " 'Then I will declare to them,' " Jesus said, " ' "I never knew you; depart from Me, you who practice lawlessness" ' " (Matthew 7:23). If Jesus abolished the law, why would He so strongly warn against lawlessness?

The Greek word that Matthew used here for *lawlessness* is the same one John used when he wrote that "whoever commits sin also commits lawlessness, and sin is lawlessness" (1 John 3:4). How could Jesus warn against sin (" 'If your right eye causes you to sin, pluck it out' " [Matthew 5:29]) if He came to abolish the law that defines sin? He couldn't. And that is why He never nullified the Ten Commandments.

Sin killed Christ on the cross. Why, then, would His death allow Christians to continue in it, especially when "He was manifested to take away our sins" (1 John 3:5)? Grace is forgiveness of sin, not a license to practice it. Can any serious Christian believe that because of the cross, he can now use the Lord's name in vain, worship idols, steal, murder, or dishonor his parents?

Danny, no matter how sincere, didn't really mean what he said. He meant that Jesus abolished the *Sabbath commandment*, not all ten. But to be consistent, he wiped them all out. How often, in an attempt to get around the fourth commandment, do Christians annul all ten, without understanding the implications.

I wonder what Danny's response would have been had I asked, "Then, can I have your wife tonight?"

Would he have replied, "Of course, Jesus abolished the Ten Commandments"?

I don't think so.

25

When Jesus became a human, Israel had been under the bondage of many great powers in the ancient Near East. Despite the prophets' promises that Israel would triumph gloriously over her enemies, the Jews had been subjugated by one nation after another. Reading the prophets, the leaders saw that one reason Israel had not seen the promised glory was because their fathers had desecrated the Sabbath. So the Jewish leaders determined not to repeat that mistake.

However, as Walter Harrelson notes, "the Hebrew Bible offers no specifications as to what one is supposed to do on the Sabbath."[33] This ambiguity wasn't true just of the Sabbath, but of other religious issues as well. In response, the rabbis developed a large body of Halakha (law) about every aspect of Judaism, including the Sabbath.

For centuries, the scholars refused to write down these laws, fearful that they would be treated as Scripture. Eventually, the laws became so extensive that they had to be written down. These codified laws developed into the Talmud, a collection of sixty-three books, or "tractates," covering Jewish life. Two tractates, *Shabbath* and *Erubin*, deal specifically with the Sabbath, and it is touched on in others as well. *Shabbath* is the longest tractate.

As the Talmud shows, the Jews loved the Sabbath and tried to heed the biblical command to call it " 'a delight' " (Isaiah 58:13). Unfortunately, in their zeal they bogged down in an endless parade of details on the minutest subjects.

The Jew, for example, couldn't squeeze fruit to press out the juice on the Sabbath; even if the juice came out by itself, he was forbidden to use it.[34] On the Sabbath, a corpse could be anointed and washed as long as its limbs weren't moved; if, however, a loaf of bread or a child was placed on it, the corpse could be moved, but only within the confines of the house.[35] If a deer wandered into a home, it was unlawful for one man, but not for two, to trap it.[36] The Jew was not allowed to search his garment for vermin on the Sabbath,[37] nor could a Jew eat an egg that had been laid on the Sabbath.[38] On the Sabbath, a man was not to carry a stone, but he could carry a child who held a stone.[39] Also, on the basis of one verse in Deuteronomy, the scholars prohibited thirty-nine classes of work on the Sabbath, such as sowing, plowing, reaping, winnowing, hunting a gazelle, kneading, baking, grinding, sifting, and washing.[40]

These rules evolved over the centuries, codified only by the fifth century A.D. Which specific ones were enforced at the time of Jesus is hard to tell. What's easy to tell is that the Sabbath by then had become so burdened down with man-made rules that the Pharisees lost sight not only of its purpose, but of its Lord as well.

26

The Greek word *sabbaton* occurs sixty-seven times in the New Testament, meaning either "Sabbath" or "week." Fifty-six of those sixty-seven times, the word appears in the Gospels, and of those, fifty refer to the Sabbath day itself. Thus, by far, more is written about the Sabbath in the Gospels than in the rest of the New Testament combined.

This point should not be overlooked. The Gospels are not merely historical books, though they contain history; nor are they merely biographies of Jesus, though of course they contain His biography. Rather, they are "theological handbooks of the early church"[41] used to promote Christianity and teach doctrine, including, apparently (because of so many references to it), the doctrine of the Sabbath.

Was Jesus in the Gospels abolishing the Sabbath? Was He instituting another day? Or was He teaching people how to keep it properly? These questions get to the crux of the Sabbath issue in the New Testament, especially in the Gospels.

Early on, the Gospels show that Jesus Himself kept the Sabbath.

"He came to Nazareth, where He had been brought up. And *as His custom was*, He went into the synagogue on the Sabbath day, and stood up to read" (Luke 4:16, emphasis supplied).

This is one of numerous verses that place Jesus in the synagogue on Sabbath, "as His custom was."[42] Obviously, Jesus was a Sabbath keeper.

The common argument is that Jesus kept the Sabbath because

He was Jewish, and therefore His example doesn't apply to Christians.

But the Sabbath, as shown previously, *was not Jewish*. Originally, the day had nothing to do with the Jews. It predated them by centuries, even millennia. Jesus kept the Sabbath, not because He was Jewish, but because it was a commandment from God, and Jesus said, "I have kept My Father's commandments" (John 15:10).

Had Jesus lived in Roman Catholic Ireland instead of being born into Jewish Palestine, He still would have kept the seventh-day Sabbath, just as He would the commandment forbidding murder. Why? Because had He broken any of the commandments, including the Sabbath, He would have sinned. And had He sinned, He would not have been the "lamb without blemish and without spot" (1 Peter 1:19) needed to atone for our sin.

Instead, "He [God] made Him who knew no sin [Jesus] to be sin for us, that we might become the righteousness of God in Him" (2 Corinthians 5:21). If Jesus had transgressed the fourth commandment, or any other, He could not have been our perfect substitute. Instead, He would have needed a Saviour as the rest of us do because He would have been a sinner as the rest of us are.

Jesus kept the Sabbath commandment for the same reason He kept the one forbidding adultery: not because either was specifically Jewish, but because to disobey would have been sin, and Jesus never sinned.

Also, Jesus kept the Sabbath not only on earth as a human being in Jewish flesh, but He kept it as Creator as well. The fourth commandment is the only one that the Lord, before His incarnation, is recorded as having Himself obeyed. "On the seventh day God ended His work which He had done, and *He rested on the seventh day from all His work which He had done*" (Genesis 2:2, emphasis supplied).

Scripture, therefore, depicts Jesus keeping the Sabbath, both in His role as Creator and as Redeemer. Interesting, too, that the themes of creation and redemption are found together only in the Sabbath commandment.

27

In the Gospels, the Sabbath usually appears in the context of controversy, with Jesus or His disciples accused of violating the fourth commandment. One conflict, recorded in three accounts (see Matthew 12:1-8; Mark 2:23-28; Luke 6:1-5), deals with the disciples plucking some heads of wheat to eat and "rubbing them in their hands" on the Sabbath (Luke 6:1).

" 'Look,' " declared the Pharisees, " 'Your disciples are doing what is not lawful to do on the Sabbath!' " (Matthew 12:2).

Who said? Jews were allowed to pluck grain from a field (see Deuteronomy 23:25), and nothing in the Bible prohibited that act on Sabbath.

"Ransack the Torah as you will," wrote D. A. Carson, and "it remains difficult to see what law was broken by the disciples."[43] There were biblical restrictions on harvesting and preparing food on the Sabbath, but, as Carson wrote, "the disciples are neither farmers or housewives trying to slip in a little overtime on the sly."[44] Instead, they were merely hungry people eating on Sabbath. The issue is not whether the disciples broke a biblical command, which they didn't, but whether they broke a man-made regulation, which they did.

Jesus responded by referring to David, who, with his men, " 'ate the showbread, which is not lawful to eat' " (Mark 2:26). In other words, "if it was right for David and his hungry companions to eat the holy bread belonging to the priests," wrote Walter Specht, "how much more could the hungry disciples violate the scribal rules about the sacred Sabbath."[45]

Jesus then summarized the essence of His view of the Sabbath in contrast to that of the Pharisees. " 'The Sabbath was made for man,' " He said, " 'and not man for the Sabbath' " (Mark 2:27).

The leaders had so weighed down the day with man-made prohibitions that, instead of freeing Israel every week, the seventh day bound them in chains. Rather than being a delight, a joy, and a blessing, as it was intended, the day had become such a burden that people weren't allowed even to pluck a little grain and eat if hungry.

" 'If you had known what this means,' " Jesus said to the Pharisees, " ' "I desire mercy and not sacrifice," you would not have condemned the guiltless' " (Matthew 12:7). Obsessed with their petty rules, the Pharisees neglected the weightier matters of the law, such as justice, mercy, and faith. Intending to protect the sanctity of the Sabbath and make it a delight, they had defiled and ruined it instead, because the rules had become an end in themselves.

Then, asserting His divine authority, Jesus declared, " 'The Son of Man is also Lord of the Sabbath' " (Luke 6:5). As Creator and Redeemer, Jesus had the final word regarding the Sabbath. As the One who created all things (see Colossians 1:16), including the Sabbath (see Genesis 2:2), Jesus was the Lord of the Sabbath. It was His prerogative, not the scribes' or Pharisees' role, to determine what was lawful on His holy day—and plucking grain to satisfy hunger was.

Jesus was attempting to turn the Jews away from the pharisaical legalism of the Sabbath, not from the Sabbath itself. Also, why would He have faced all this trouble from the rabbis over the Sabbath if it was His intention eventually to abrogate it?

Nowhere in this story did Jesus even intimate that the day was to be changed to Sunday. The issue was not which day was to be kept (obviously it's the seventh), but *how*. If He was pointing His disciples toward the first day instead of the seventh, He didn't here. Indeed, the first day of the week wasn't even mentioned.

28

The Jews saw in the Sabbath, and correctly so, a preview of Messianic redemption. Jewish laws, writes Theodore Freidman, "give voice to the idea that the Sabbath is the anticipation, the foretaste, the paradigm of life in the world-to-come. The abundance of such statements is the surest evidence of how deeprooted and widespread that notion was in early rabbinic literature."[46] As a result of this understanding, scholars decided that whatever would not be done in the *'olam ha-ba* (the Messianic world to come) should not be done on Sabbath, the preview of the *'olam ha-ba*.

One rabbinic school, for instance, taught that a person should not search his garments for vermin on Sabbath because he might kill them, and killing would not occur in the world to come.[47]

Because no sickness or death would be in the *'olam ha-ba*, the Jews were not to mourn the dead on Sabbath, conduct funerals, or even visit the sick. Also, if no sickness would exist in the *'olam ha-ba*, no healings would either. This concept probably motivated the Pharisees' opposition to Christ's Sabbath healings.

Whether casting out demons (see Luke 4:31-37), giving sight to the blind (see John 9), or reconstructing a withered hand (see Matthew 12:9-14), Jesus ministered to the sick and infirm on the Sabbath. As with the plucking of grain, no biblical command forbade Sabbath healing. Far from violating the Sabbath, Christ, by His words and deeds, restored its true purpose.

" 'Is it lawful on the Sabbath,' " Jesus asked the Pharisees, " 'to do good or to do evil, to save life or to kill?' " (Mark 3:4).

On another Sabbath, after curing a man with dropsy, Jesus confronted His accusers: " 'Which of you, having a donkey or an ox that has fallen into a pit, will not immediately pull him out on the Sabbath day?' " (Luke 14:5). When attacked by the leaders for healing a woman on Sabbath, Jesus responded, " 'Hypocrite! Does not each one of you on the Sabbath loose his ox or his donkey from the stall, and lead it away to water it? So ought not this woman, being a daughter of Abraham, whom Satan has bound—think of it—for eighteen years, be loosed from this bond on the Sabbath?' " (Luke 13:15, 16).

In all His Sabbath healings, Jesus wasn't superseding the Sabbath, setting it aside, or nullifying it. Rather, He was clarifying an aspect of the Sabbath that had been turned on its head. Because Sabbath *did* preview Messianic redemption, what better time to display a taste of the freedom, healing, and liberty that this redemption promises? What better time to give a foretaste of the ultimate redemption in the *'olam ha-ba*? Far from being a day *not* to heal the sick, the Sabbath was the most appropriate day on which to do it.

It was on the Sabbath that Jesus publicly announced His mission " 'to heal the brokenhearted, to preach deliverance to the captives and recovery of sight to the blind, to set at liberty those who are oppressed, to preach the acceptable year of the Lord' " (Luke 4:18, 19), and it was on the Sabbath as well that Jesus went about these tasks.

Never did He question the validity of the day. Jesus didn't heal on Sabbath so that men would abandon the seventh day and substitute a new one. He never mentioned another day, much less the first day of the week, in any of His Sabbath healing accounts. Jesus hadn't violated the Sabbath by healing on it. Jacob Jervell wrote that "there is no conflict with the law in Jesus' attitude as described in many disputes about the Sabbath. Luke records no less than four disputes and he is concerned to show that Jesus acted in complete accordance with the law, and that the Jewish leaders were not able to raise any objections."[48] Nothing Jesus did or said lessened the obligation to keep the seventh-day Sabbath.

If anything, the fact that the Holy Spirit inspired the Gospel writers to spend so much time recording the Sabbath controversies and Christ's lessons regarding proper Sabbath keeping points to the Sabbath's continued importance for the church.

Christ's own words prove that importance. Warning His disciples to flee when the Roman armies besieged Jerusalem, Jesus said, " 'Pray that your flight may not be in winter or on the Sabbath' " (Matthew 24:20).

Much speculation has gone into the reason for this warning. Some have suggested that the gates of Jerusalem would be shut on Sabbath, which is why Jesus told His followers to pray that their flight would be on another day. A few verses earlier, however, Jesus said, " 'Let those who are *in Judea* flee to the mountains' " (verse 16, emphasis supplied); the closing of the city gates, therefore, had no significance for them, yet Jesus gave them warning anyway. Whatever Christ's specific motive, His words undeniably show that "our Lord expected His followers to regard the Sabbath as sacred as late as A.D. 70."[49]

No wonder D. A. Carson, though arguing for Sunday worship, admits, "There is not a hint anywhere in the ministry of Jesus that the first day of the week is to take on the character of Sabbath and replace it."[50]

Christ's words in Matthew 24, as everywhere else in the Gospels, don't prove that Jesus had transferred the Sabbath to the first day of the week. Jesus never even mentioned the first day of the week, so He could have hardly instituted the change.

29

Many Christians believe that the first day of the week, instead of replacing the Sabbath, "was chosen to commemorate the unique, salvation-historical event of the death and resurrection of Christ."[51] A look at *all* the New Testament references to the first day of the week will show whether the first day, Sunday, was to replace or commemorate anything.

The Gospel of Mark mentions the first day of the week only twice. Mark says, "Now when the Sabbath was past, Mary Magdalene, Mary the mother of James, and Salome bought spices, that they might come and anoint Him. Very early in the morning, on the first day of the week, they came to the tomb when the sun had risen. . . . Now when He rose early on the first day of the week, He appeared first to Mary Magdalene" (Mark 16:1, 2, 9).

The morning of the first day of the week, when Jesus rose, was Sunday. Though written more than twenty-five years after the cross, Mark's Gospel never hints that Sunday had replaced Sabbath. On the contrary, Mark describes the first day *in contrast* to Sabbath; he says that the "Sabbath was past" before the first day of the week began.

Matthew has this to say about the first day of the week. "Now after the Sabbath, as the first day of the week began to dawn, Mary Magdalene and the other Mary came to see the tomb" (Matthew 28:1). Matthew never talks about the first day of the week again. His was the most popular Gospel of the early church, the one most often quoted by early Christians writers, yet Mat-

thew says nothing about the first day of the week either superseding or replacing Sabbath, even though his Gospel has been
dated from the late 60s to 80 A.D.

Luke wrote in his Gospel that after the crucifixion, the women
"rested on the Sabbath according to the commandment. Now on
the first day of the week, very early in the morning, they, and
certain other women with them, came to the tomb bringing the
spices which they had prepared" (Luke 23:56–24:1). These followers of Jesus had never been taught to abandon the seventh-
day Sabbath; rather, as Luke pointed out, they observed it. Luke,
writing about the same time as Matthew, never hints that the first
day replaced the seventh.

Here is what John says about the first day of the week. "On
the first day of the week Mary Magdalene came to the tomb early,
while it was still dark, and saw that the stone had been taken
away" (John 20:1). Again, as in the other Gospels, John doesn't
call the first day holy or sanctified. Rather, he mentions it only
as part of the chronology of Christ's death and resurrection.

He continues, "Then, the same day at evening, being the first
day of the week, when the doors were shut where the disciples
were assembled, for fear of the Jews, Jesus came and stood in the
midst, and said to them, 'Peace be with you' " (verse 19). This
verse, often used to promote Sunday worship, mentions nothing
about a worship service in honor of Christ's resurrection; rather,
it says only that the disciples had assembled behind locked doors
"for fear of the Jews." Locked doors hardly sound like a religious
service! Except for Mary's testimony, the disciples didn't even
know for certain that Jesus had been resurrected. Not until He
appeared, showing them "His hands and His side" (verse 20) did
they know for sure that He had been resurrected, so they were
hardly assembled to celebrate that event.

John's silence on the sanctity of the first day remains significant because his Gospel was written toward the end of the first
century, when the change of the Sabbath was supposedly instituted. John, like Matthew, Mark, and Luke, knew nothing about
the first day being sacred, but he, like them, does have much to
say about proper Sabbath keeping, with Jesus as the example.

If the holy Sabbath day had been changed to Sunday, surely

Matthew, Mark, and John—all Jews whose forefathers had kept the Sabbath for more than a millennium—should have written something about it. In their Gospels, however, they wrote nothing about such a change, either by the transfer of Sabbath to Sunday or by Sunday superseding the Sabbath. This silence is strange because, if Christ instituted such a major change, wouldn't these founders of His church have said *something*?

30

The book of Acts repeatedly records that the followers of Christ, after Calvary, worshiped publicly on Sabbath even in Gentile lands (see Acts 13:5, 14, 42; 16:13; 17:2; 18:4; 19:8, etc.), while it mentions the first day of the week only once.

"Now on the first day of the week, when the disciples came together to break bread, Paul, ready to depart the next day, spoke to them and continued his message until midnight" (Acts 20:7).

Many believe that because this verse talks about "breaking bread," it is referring to a worship service and the celebration of the Lord's Supper on the new Christian Sabbath, Sunday, the Lord's Day.

Is this true?

First, of the fifteen times that the phrase *to break bread* appears in the New Testament (in various verbal conjugations), it refers to the Lord's Supper only twice. The majority of references deal merely with eating. Acts 2:46, for example, talks about the followers of Christ "continuing *daily* with one accord in the temple, and *breaking bread* from house to house, *they ate their food* with gladness and simplicity of heart" (emphasis supplied). "Breaking bread" here doesn't mean the Lord's Supper; it simply means eating meals.

Also, Acts 20 suggests that Paul is breaking bread alone: "When he had come up, had broken bread and eaten . . . he departed" (verse 11). The verbs are singular, so Paul is obviously not participating in a *communion* service, and nothing in the whole section ever mentions wine.

But the text does indicate a Sunday worship service in the early Christian church, doesn't it?

If Luke used the Jewish (sundown to sundown) reckoning of days, this evening assembly on the first day of the week would actually have been on Saturday night (Paul talked "even till daybreak" [verse 11]). The New English Bible even translates the phrase as "Saturday night" (verse 7).

Even if Paul used Roman (midnight to midnight) reckoning, so that this meeting took place on Sunday night, it hardly sounds like a weekly worship service. The context suggests that this was a special all-night meeting because Paul was to depart in the morning. As historian Augustus Neander wrote, "the impending departure of the apostle, may have united the little Church in a brotherly parting-meal, on the occasion of which the apostle delivered his last address, although there was no particular celebration of a Sunday in the case."[52]

And finally, nothing in this verse even hints that the first day has either replaced or superseded Sabbath.

In all the rest of the New Testament, the first day of the week appears only once, when Paul wrote to the Corinthians about a relief offering for poor church members in Jerusalem and Judea. "On the first day of the week let each one of you lay something aside, storing up as he may prosper, that there be no collections when I come" (1 Corinthians 16:2). Does this verse prove Sunday sacredness?

As with every other New Testament reference to the first day, this verse says nothing about the first day being sacred or holy. It isn't talking about a public worship service in which offerings are brought. It isn't even talking about worship. Rather, Paul admonishes each believer to "lay something aside, storing [it] up," probably in their own homes.

As F. W. Grosheide comments: "Paul trusts the Corinthians: he does not ask them to hand in their collection on a weekly basis, they are allowed to keep the collected money and thus little by little a significant amount will be saved up."[53] Much speculation has gone into why Paul specified the first day of the week as the time for figuring and setting aside one's offering. Some have suggested that the first day of the week was pay day, or perhaps they were to reckon this offering as the secular week began "before the demands of secular life could absorb the week's earnings."[54] Whatever the reason, the verse says nothing about Sunday being a sacred day of worship.

But what about Revelation 1:10, where John wrote, "I was in the Spirit on the Lord's Day"? Doesn't that prove Sunday worship in the early church?

How could it? No New Testament reference to the first day ever gives Sunday a sacred character or ever calls it the Lord's Day. Just because Sunday has been called the Lord's Day for years doesn't make it the Lord's Day, any more than the fact that people believed for centuries that the earth was the center of the universe makes it so. We shouldn't read *back* into this phrase the meaning of Sunday. Instead, we should use the Bible to read *into* the phrase its *biblical* meaning, and nothing in Scripture ever calls the first day of the week the Lord's Day.

Another point—John's Gospel is usually dated later than Revelation. Why would John in his Gospel call Sunday merely "the first day of the week," if, in an earlier book, Revelation, he had already referred to it as the Lord's Day?

Scripture actually points to the seventh-day Sabbath as "the Lord's Day." In the Ten Commandments the seventh day is called " 'the Sabbath *of the Lord your God*' " (Exodus 20:10, emphasis supplied). In Isaiah, the Lord calls it " 'My holy day' " (Isaiah 58:13). In three Gospels, Jesus calls Himself " 'Lord even of the Sabbath' " (see Matthew 12:8; Mark 2:28; Luke 6:5). Jesus is, therefore, the Lord of the Sabbath day. It is His, the Lord Jesus', day.

Or simply, the Lord's Day.

31

Of the nine New Testament verses commonly used to prove Sunday worship, only eight even refer to Sunday. Of those, as we have seen, six deal only with the chronology regarding the discovery of Christ's empty tomb or with the day Christians in one city set aside a special offering. Of the two remaining texts, one talks about believers hiding after the death of their Master; the other refers to an all-night assembly with the apostle Paul. Despite the sincere belief of many good Christians, none of these texts speaks of a worship service on Sunday or gives any evidence that Sunday has either replaced or superseded the seventh-day Sabbath.

Many Christians admit this. Writing in *The Lord's Day*, a book published to promote Sunday as the Christian Sabbath, Samuel A. Cartledge says that "we must admit that we can point to no direct command that we cease observing the seventh day and begin using the first day."[55]

In the same book, Donald C. McHenry admits, "The Sunday we hold sacred was not commanded by Jesus."[56]

In the introduction to *From Sabbath to Lord's Day*, a large scholarly tome devoted to the promotion of Sunday, D. A. Carson writes, "We are not persuaded that the New Testament unambiguously develops a 'transfer theology,' according to which the Sabbath moves from the seventh day to the first day of the week."[57]

Concerning the change of Sabbath to Sunday, James Wesberry, executive director of the Lord's Day Alliance, an organization devoted to promotion of Sunday worship, confesses, "There is no record of a statement on the part of Jesus authorizing such a change, nor is there recorded such a statement on the part of the apostles."[58]

Harold Lindsell, in *Christianity Today*, writes, "There is nothing in Scripture that requires us to keep Sunday rather than Saturday as a holy day."[59]

Many earnest Christians, however, believe that the key to understanding Sunday sacredness appears in the writings of Paul. This is surprising because the only time the apostle ever mentions the first day of the week is 1 Corinthians 16:1, 2— verses that say nothing about Sunday as a holy day.

Nevertheless, because Paul is often quoted in the Sabbath-Sunday dialogue, we need to look at the verses commonly used. One verse, not used but that should be, comes from Peter, when he talks about some of Paul's epistles. Peter warns that in some places in his letters, Paul is "speaking in them of these things, in which are some things hard to understand, which those who are untaught and unstable twist to their own destruction, as they do also the rest of the Scriptures" (2 Peter 3:16). Thus, Peter warns that some of Paul's writings are hard to understand and that some people twist him, even to "their own destruction."

These harder things of Paul can be more easily understood, however, by always interpreting Paul in the light of Jesus. Why? Because Paul wrote that "the gospel which was preached by me is not according to man. For I neither received it from man, nor was I taught it, but it came through the revelation of Jesus Christ" (Galatians 1:11, 12). Having received the truth from Jesus Christ directly, Paul wasn't going to teach anything opposed to what Christ taught him, and Jesus wasn't going to teach Paul anything opposed to what He Himself taught. Therefore, many of the difficult things in Paul can make more sense if we interpret them in light of the simple sayings of Jesus. Meanwhile, any interpretation of Paul that contradicts Jesus is, we can be sure, a misinterpretation.

32

Early in my quest for truth, sincere Christians would quote Pauline verses such as "You are not under law but under grace" (Romans 6:14), or "Man is justified by faith apart from the deeds of the law" (Romans 3:28) in an attempt to turn me away from the Sabbath. Obviously, they didn't grasp the implications of their theology. Had I asked about the commandments against adultery, murder, or taking the name of the Lord in vain, these verses wouldn't have come from their lips. But even if they had applied the verses they quoted to *all* the commandments, it would have made no difference, because the verses don't teach that obedience to the law is not important for the Christian. They simply teach that obedience does not save us.

According to the Bible, we have all sinned, we have all broken God's law, we are all condemned by that law, and therefore we all deserve to die an eternal death, "for the wages of sin is death" (Romans 6:23). But Jesus, who lived in perfect obedience to that law, has Himself paid the penalty for our transgression of it. "God demonstrates His own love toward us, in that while we were still sinners, Christ died for us" (Romans 5:8). Therefore, because of what He has done for us, we don't have to pay the penalty, when we accept by faith His sacrifice in our behalf. By accepting the sacrifice of Jesus on the cross, we can be "justified freely by His grace through the redemption that is in Christ Jesus" (Romans 3:24).

When we admit, confess, and repent of our sin, and then give ourselves totally and unreservedly to Jesus, accepting by faith

His perfect righteousness in our behalf—we stand before God pardoned, forgiven, and accepted as if we, like Jesus, had never sinned. We are accepted, not because of what we have done but because of what Jesus has done for us. This is justification by faith, and it is the best of all good news.

Jesus Himself taught it in what is probably the most well-known verse in the Bible: " 'For God so loved the world that He gave His only begotten Son, that whoever believes in Him should not perish but have everlasting life' " (John 3:16). Paul later put it this way, "Therefore, having been justified by faith, we have peace with God through our Lord Jesus Christ" (Romans 5:1). The Greek word translated *believes* in John 3:16 comes from the same root as the word Paul used for *faith* in Romans 5:1. So we can interchange the words as follows: "For God so loved the world that He gave His only begotten Son, that whoever *has faith* in Him should not perish but have everlasting life." "Therefore having been justified by *belief* in Him, we have peace with God through our Lord Jesus Christ."

Because salvation comes only through faith in Christ, and not by works of the law, Paul declared that he wanted to be found in Jesus, "not having my own righteousness, which is from the law, but that which is through faith in Christ, the righteousness which is from God by faith" (Philippians 3:9).

Although Paul stressed that we cannot be saved by the law, he insisted that we are still obliged to obey it, for "sin is the transgression of the law" (1 John 3:4, KJV). In fact, born-again, saved Christians are the only ones who can truly keep God's law. Only they have the promise of Christ working in them (see Philippians 1:6). And without that power from Jesus, no one can keep God's law. The gospel was never meant to excuse sin, but to save from its consequences and grip.

After explaining how the law, in and of itself, cannot save us, Paul writes, "What shall we say then? Is the law sin? Certainly not! On the contrary, I would not have known sin except through the law. For I would not have known covetousness unless the law had said, 'You shall not covet' " (Romans 7:7).

It's as if Paul foresaw how some would misunderstand what he wrote about law and faith. Almost always, after asserting that salvation is by faith alone, Paul adds the reminder that faith doesn't allow for transgression. After explaining that "sin shall not have dominion over you, for you are not under law but under grace" (Romans 6:14), he immediately adds, "What then? Shall we sin because we are not under law but under grace? Certainly not!" (verse 15).

Paul is clear that works do not save us. " 'Knowing that a man is not justified by the works of the law but by faith in Jesus Christ, even we have believed in Christ Jesus, that we might be justified by faith in Christ and not by the works of the law; for by the works of the law no flesh shall be justified' " (Galatians 2:16). Yet, afraid this truth could be misconstrued into belief that Christians are free to disobey that law, he continues, " 'But if, while we seek to be justified by Christ, we ourselves also are found sinners, is Christ therefore a minister of sin? Certainly not!' " (verse 17).

No wonder Paul wrote that "circumcision is nothing and uncircumcision is nothing, but keeping the commandments of God is what matters" (1 Corinthians 7:19).

While law cannot save, Paul knew people would not be saved in blatant transgression of it. "Not the hearers of the law are just in the sight of God, but the doers of the law will be justified" (Romans 2:13).

" 'Honor your father and mother,' " Paul commanded, "which is the first commandment with promise" (Ephesians 6:2). If he believed in the *fifth* commandment, what makes anyone think he abolished the *fourth*?

My Christian friends talked about the new covenant, which they said changed, or even abolished, the law—so Christians didn't have to keep the fourth commandment.

" 'Behold, the days are coming,' says the Lord, 'when I will make a new covenant with the house of Israel and with the house of Judah. . . . For this is the covenant that I will make with the house of Israel: After those days,' says the Lord, 'I will put My laws in their mind and write them on their hearts' " (Hebrews 8:8, 10).

In the new covenant, God will write His law on our hearts and minds. The covenant is new, not His law! Under the new covenant, God writes His law in the minds and hearts of His people, so obviously the law is not abolished.

"Therefore the law is holy," Paul wrote, "and the commandment holy and just and good" (Romans 7:12). The law *is* holy, it *is* just, it *is* good. It just can't save us. Only Jesus can save us, if we accept Him by faith.

It's true, as my Christian friends always quoted, that "a man is justified by faith apart from the deeds of the law" (Romans 3:28). They forgot, however, Paul's words a few verses later: "Do we then make void the law through faith? Certainly not! On the contrary, we establish the law" (verse 31).

33

If Paul, like Jesus, upheld the Ten Commandments, did Paul, like Jesus, keep the Sabbath as well?

In the book of Acts, Luke puts Paul in the synagogue on Sabbath "as his custom was," the same phrase Luke used to describe Christ's Sabbath keeping (Acts 17:2; cf. Luke 4:16). The events of Acts, as well as the writing of the book itself, happened years, even decades, after the cross. If Sabbath had been changed to Sunday, why didn't Luke, the only *Gentile* writer in the New Testament, record the change?

Instead, Acts repeatedly describes Paul preaching on the Sabbath in the synagogues—not only to Jews, but to Gentiles as well. In Pisidian Antioch, for example, after Paul talked in the synagogue, "the Gentiles begged that these words might be preached to them the next Sabbath. . . . And the next Sabbath almost the whole city came together to hear the word of God" (Acts 13:42, 44). In Corinth, Paul "reasoned in the synagogue every Sabbath, and persuaded both *Jews and Greeks*" (Acts 18:4, emphasis supplied).

In Philippi, Luke switches from third to first person, writing that "on the Sabbath day we went out of the city to the riverside, where prayer was customarily made; and we sat down and spoke to the women who met there" (Acts 16:13). This Sabbath meeting wasn't even in a synagogue, but beside the river. A woman "who worshiped God" (a phrase for a Gentile attracted to Judaism) accepted Christ at this Sabbath meeting (see verses 14, 15).

In none of these instances does Paul attempt to turn his

converts, even the Gentiles, away from the seventh day in favor of the first. If something as radical as the change of the Sabbath had occurred, it surely would have been mentioned.

As more Gentiles joined the fledgling movement, some Jewish believers insisted that these Gentiles be circumcised and keep the law of Moses (see Acts 15:1, 5). But after a meeting in Jerusalem, Paul and the other disciples concluded that the Gentile converts were " 'to abstain from things polluted by idols, from sexual immorality, from things strangled, and from blood' " (verse 20).

Some misconstrue this verse to mean that these few prohibitions were *all* the Gentiles believers were required to obey. If true, were the Gentiles allowed to steal, lie, murder, and use the Lord's name in vain because these weren't specifically prohibited by the council?

Rather, the issue simply deals with practices among Gentiles that would offend their Jewish brethren in the faith. "What the Jerusalem council laid down," wrote Walter Specht, "was the terms for fellowship between Jewish and Gentile Christians."[60] Certain practices, often prevalent among Gentiles, but scandalous to Jews, were singled out and prohibited, but certainly not at the exclusion of the Ten Commandments.

The fact that the Jerusalem Council did not specifically mention the Sabbath as something binding on the Gentiles (neither did it mention theft or murder), far from hinting at its abolition, helps prove the opposite. Had a movement to abolish or change the day been prevalent, then the Jews who were already arguing for circumcision and obedience to the law of Moses certainly would have made an issue of the sacred seventh-day Sabbath as well! Instead, the silence testifies that Sabbath observance by the Gentiles wasn't even questioned, perhaps because many of the Gentile converts already were going to the synagogue on Sabbath, as the book of Acts indicates.

Paul would sometimes address his congregation as "men of Israel, *and you who fear God*" (Acts 13:16, emphasis supplied) or "men and brethren, sons of the family of Abraham, *and those among you who fear God*" (verse 26, emphasis supplied). Those who "feared God" were Gentiles attracted to Judaism. Acts often mentions such Gentiles who already believed in the Jewish faith before learning about Jesus (see Acts 10:1, 2, 22; 16:14; 17:7; 18:7). Such believers obviously knew of the Sabbath, and it was among these that Paul often had his greatest success.

Almost two thousand years ago, Jewish historian Flavius Josephus wrote, "There is not a city of the Grecians nor any of the barbarians, nor any nation whatsoever, whither our custom of resting on the seventh day hath not come."[61] For converts to Judaism, Sabbath keeping was already known, which is probably why it never became an issue in the early Christian church.

34

Another verse used against Sabbath keeping is found in Romans 14:1-6:

> Receive one who is weak in the faith, but not to disputes over doubtful things. For one believes he may eat all things, but he who is weak eats only vegetables. Let not him who eats despise him who does not eat, and let not him who does not eat judge him who eats; for God has received him. Who are you to judge another's servant? To his own master he stands or falls. . . . *One person esteems one day above another; another esteems every day alike. Let each be fully convinced in his own mind. He who observes the day, observes it to the Lord; and he who does not observe the day, to the Lord he does not observe it.* He who eats, eats to the Lord, for he gives God thanks; and he who does not eat, to the Lord he does not eat, and gives God thanks (emphasis supplied).

Paul's basic attitude here seems to be *"Do what you want; just don't judge each other."* It hardly sounds as if he's dealing with one of the Ten Commandments. Remember that in another place Paul said, "Circumcision is nothing and uncircumcision is nothing, but keeping the commandments of God is what matters" (1 Corinthians 7:19). Can we imagine him taking the attitude that the commandments of God are merely a matter of personal preference—especially when Jesus, his Lord, took the commandments so seriously He warned that lust is adultery and anger is murder?

The original question with which Paul is dealing in these verses isn't even about the law of Moses, which specified clean and unclean meats, but with vegetarianism. Therefore, Paul is discussing a problem *outside of biblical law*. Some believers, whom Paul labels "weak," ate only vegetables, while some of their fellow believers ate other things as well. Then, almost as an afterthought, Paul talks about those who esteem one day better than another, while some esteem all days alike. He handles this question in the same manner as vegetarianism. *"If you want to eat only vegies, fine; if not, fine. If you want to esteem one day over another, fine; if not, fine."* Is it realistic to think that Paul, in one breath, could go from vegetarianism, not a biblical issue, to the fourth commandment, saying Christians should do whatever they want in either, especially when a few chapters earlier he had said that "the law is holy, and the commandment holy and just and good" (Romans 7:12)? Obviously not. The "days" in these verses have nothing to do with the seventh-day Sabbath.

Because the context concerns food, scholars have suggested that the "days" Paul is speaking of here were most likely religious fast days. Many of the early believers were devout Jews, and fasting was a part of their religion. Paul would more likely say "Let each one be convinced in his own mind" over arbitrary, nonessential fast days than he would over the biblical command to keep the seventh-day Sabbath, especially when he himself was a Sabbath keeper, as was also his Lord Jesus.

35

Another common Pauline verse erroneously used to discredit Sabbath keeping is Colossians 2:16, 17, which reads: "Let no one judge you in food or in drink, or regarding a festival or a new moon or sabbaths, which are a shadow of things to come, but the substance is of Christ." Does this verse prove that Christians should no longer keep the Sabbath day?

As always, context is crucial. Paul is writing to the Colossians, who were keeping numerous regulations, many man-made: "Therefore, if you died with Christ from the basic principles of the world, why, as though living in the world, do you subject yourselves to regulations—'Do not touch, do not taste, do not handle,' which all concern things which perish with the using—*according to the commandments and doctrines of men*?" (Colossians 2:20-22, emphasis supplied; see also 2:8). He couldn't be talking here about the weekly Sabbath or any of the Ten Commandments, for they certainly weren't "doctrines of men."

Most commentators agree that the Colossians were mixing Jewish ceremonial laws with a pagan asceticism that included "worship of angels" (verse 18) and that had "an appearance of wisdom in self-imposed religion, false humility, and neglect of the body, but are of no value against the indulgence of the flesh" (verse 23). Whatever the Colossians were doing, Paul was not chiding them over obedience to the Ten Commandments.

As with the text in Romans we just looked at, Paul can't be dealing here with the seventh-day Sabbath. First, the festivals, new moons, and sabbaths are called a "shadow of things to come" (verse 17). The ceremonial laws, which included various yearly sabbaths, were shadows of things to come, but not the weekly seventh-day Sabbath, instituted before sin.

Verse 14 talks about how the "handwriting of requirements" was "nailed . . . to the cross." How could this verse include the seventh-day Sabbath, especially when Jesus Himself, referring to the destruction of Jerusalem that would take place almost forty years after the cross, told His followers to "pray that your flight may not be in winter *or on the Sabbath*" (Matthew 24:20, emphasis supplied). If the seventh-day Sabbath were nailed to the cross, even the Lord of the Sabbath knew nothing about it.

Also, Paul couldn't be talking about the Ten Commandments here because in the next chapter he warns the Colossians, among other things, against covetousness, idolatry, and lying (see Colossians 3:5, 9).

Methodist Adam Clarke wrote, "There is no intimation here that the *Sabbath* was done away with or that its moral use was superseded, by the introduction of Christianity."[62]

A careful look at Colossians 2:16 shows that Paul wasn't even directly condemning those who kept the festivals or new moons or sabbaths. He was merely saying, "Let no man judge you" concerning them. As in Romans, if Paul were dealing with the seventh-day Sabbath, or any one of the Ten Commandments, one can hardly imagine him taking such a lax view—not when he spoke so strongly against disobedience in other places. Instead, as in Romans, Paul was not even referring to the seventh-day Sabbath.

A similar verse is in Galatians, where Paul chided believers, saying that before they had become Christians, they "served those which by nature are not gods. But now after you have known God, or rather are known by God, how is it that you turn again to the weak and beggarly elements, to which you desire again to be in bondage? You observe days and months and seasons and years" (Galatians 4:8-10).

Did Paul call the seventh-day Sabbath one of those "weak and beggarly elements"? Of course not, unless Jesus referred to Himself as "Lord even of a weak and beggarly element."

Also, if observance of the seventh-day Sabbath brought

bondage, did the Creator, who not only instituted the Sabbath, but kept it at Creation, enter into that bondage when He observed the world's first Sabbath (see Genesis 2:2)? Or did Jesus enter into bondage when He kept the Sabbath for thirty-three years?

In Galatians, as in Romans and Colossians, Paul could not have been teaching the abrogation of God's law, especially not the fourth commandment, when Jesus Himself so adamantly taught and kept it.

36

Years ago, convinced of the importance of the seventh-day Sabbath, I shared my conviction with two charismatic Christians who, though at first persuaded, later said that Hebrews 4 nullified Sabbath keeping.

Does it?

In Hebrews 3, the author symbolizes salvation by calling it God's "rest." He uses the entrance into Canaan by the children of Israel after the Exodus to exemplify that rest. "Now with whom was He [God] angry forty years? Was it not with those who sinned, whose corpses fell in the wilderness? And to whom did He swear that they would not enter His rest, but to those who did not obey? So we see that they could not enter in because of unbelief" (verses 17-19).

The author continues the same line of thought in chapter 4. "Therefore, since a promise remains of entering His rest, let us fear lest any of you seem to have come short of it" (verse 1). He then uses the Sabbath as the symbol of another rest—the rest of salvation in Christ. "For He has spoken in a certain place of the seventh day in this way: 'And God rested on the seventh day from all His works', and again in this place: 'They shall not enter My rest.' Since therefore it remains that some must enter it, and those to whom it was first preached did not enter because of disobedience, again He designates a certain day" (verses 4-7).

Despite the failure of God's people in different times to enter into that salvation, or rest, he insists that "there remains therefore a rest for the people of God" (verse 9). Then, continuing his use of the Sabbath as a symbol of salvation, he admonishes his readers: "For he who has entered His rest has himself also ceased from his works *as God did from His*. Let us therefore be diligent to enter that rest, lest anyone fall after the same example of disobedience" (verses 10, 11, emphasis supplied).

Some say that these verses, in which the Sabbath symbolizes the ultimate "rest" in Christ, abrogate the Sabbath[63]; others insist that they admonish its observance.[64] Who is correct?

The Sabbath is shown here as a foretaste of salvation in Christ. Nothing here hints at its abrogation. On the other hand, neither is the author specifically advocating Sabbath observance. He is simply showing that the Sabbath symbolizes how Christians can rest from their own works just as God, at Creation, rested from His.

Indirectly, however, these verses do indicate the Sabbath's perpetuity. Sabbath is introduced here positively, as something good, even a symbol of rest in Christ. Such use wouldn't be likely had the Sabbath been replaced or superseded by Sunday. These verses presuppose the acceptance of the Sabbath, not an argument over it. Had it been discarded, its use here as a symbol of salvation would require some explanation or justification. Nothing of the sort appears, and this silence eloquently witnesses to the Sabbath's continued importance.

37

If Jesus taught people to obey the seventh-day Sabbath, not Sunday; if the apostles and disciples kept the Sabbath, not Sunday; if Scripture teaches that God sanctified the Sabbath, not Sunday—Why do most Christians observe Sunday, not the seventh-day Sabbath?

The answer lies in early church history. Christianity originated in the land of the Jews. Its Bible, early adherents, early leaders, even the Messiah, were all Jewish. Its Sabbath was "Jewish" too. The church was naturally associated with the Jews, and this caused problems, because Jewish rebellion against the Romans spawned widespread anti-Judaism in the Roman Empire. Already being fed to lions, the Christians didn't need this added struggle as well.

Samuele Bacchiocchi, whose Ph.D. dissertation documents the change of the Sabbath to Sunday, writes that as severe anti-Jewish sentiment arose, "many Christians did take steps to appear, especially in the imperial city, different and clearly distinct from the Jews in the eyes of the Romans. Under the emperor Hadrian (A.D. 117-138) particularly, a clear differentiation from the Jews became a more urgent necessity, due to the punitive measures taken . . . against them."[65]

And what did Christians do to disassociate themselves from the Jews? Among other things, they eased away from the obvious act of Sabbath keeping. Considering that "the Sabbath," wrote Bacchiocchi, was "not only outlawed by Hadrian's edict but also consistently attacked and ridiculed by Greek and Latin authors,

112

it should not surprise one that many Christians severed their ties with Judaism by substituting for distinctive Jewish religious observances such as the Sabbath . . . new ones."[66]

Social factors were involved too. Sunday was already an important day among those Romans who worshiped the sun. Also, with the church keeping the pagan Sunday instead of the "Jewish" Sabbath, it became easier for the pagans to join the new religion. By early in the fourth century, Sunday had become so entrenched in Christianity that Constantine the Great issued the first known blue law, ordering that "all judges, city people, and craftsmen shall rest on the venerable day of the Sun." Over the next few centuries, the Roman Catholic Church institutionalized Sunday keeping, and eventually the church took credit for the change.

"We observe Sunday instead of Saturday," one catechism explains, "because the Catholic church in the Council of Laodicea (A.D. 336) transferred the solemnity from Saturday to Sunday."[67]

"The Catholic church," says one Catholic paper, "for over one thousand years, by virtue of her divine mission, changed the day from Saturday to Sunday. The Protestant world, at its birth, found the Christian Sabbath too strongly entrenched to run counter to its existence. . . . The Christian Sabbath is therefore, to this day, the acknowledged offspring of the Catholic church."[68]

Thus, for centuries, most Christians have kept Sunday as the "Christian" Sabbath; in the strictest biblical sense, however, Sunday is neither Christian nor Sabbath.

38

Even if the New Testament Sabbath *is* Saturday, does it really matter?

When the Lord warned our first parents about the forbidden fruit or warned the antediluvians of the Flood or warned Lot about Sodom, did He mean what He said? When He promised Israel that they would return from Babylon or promised that the Messiah would come or promised that obedience would bring blessing, did He mean it? And when He ordered that the *seventh* day—not the first, the third, or the fifth—be kept as the "Sabbath of the Lord thy God," did He mean what He said as well?

Of course!

What right, then, have we to choose another day, when the Lord specifically chose the seventh?

The apparent arbitrariness of the seventh day, as opposed to any other, far from allowing us latitude to disregard it, presents the greatest reason to keep it. Unlike the day, the month, and the year—the seven-day cycle culminating on Sabbath is independent of any astronomical phenomena regarding the moon, sun, or stars. Nothing in nature gives it practical significance. While the Sabbath commandment has a distinct practical value, the specific day, *in and of itself*, doesn't. Thus, although in one sense keeping any other day could "work," keeping the *seventh* day is an act of faith par excellence.

Practical reasons exist for not stealing, killing, or committing adultery, none of which necessarily have to do with a relationship to Jesus. Atheists with moral values often refrain from these sins as well. By obeying the fourth commandment, however, the believer unquestionably enters into the vertical plane. "As the Christian takes heed of the Sabbath day and keeps it holy," writes Raoul Dederen, "he does so purely in answer to God's command, and simply because God is his Creator. Thus, the Sabbath commandment comes nearer to being a true measure of spirituality than any of the other commandments, and, as in the days of Israel of old, it is often more of a test of loyalty to God than is any of the others."[69]

Those who keep the seventh day, as opposed to any other, don't do so from any specific practical purpose; on the contrary, in today's Sunday-oriented society, keeping Sabbath "demands a radical, conscious, deliberate decision to follow Christ."[70] Christians who keep the seventh day do it for the most fundamental reason—because God commands them to. For those saved by God's grace alone, what other reason is needed?

39

Of course, Sabbath keeping can become a legalistic trap. The Pharisees hung Jesus on a cross and then ran home to keep His Sabbath. They knew the Sabbath but not its Lord. Nevertheless, as Robert Shuler writes, "the keeping of the seventh day by a renewed soul is not legalism, nor is it contrary to salvation by grace. In fact, the Sabbath commandment is the only precept in the law that stands as a sign of deliverance from sin and sanctification by grace alone."[71]

Though made originally only as a sign of Creation, after the Fall, the Sabbath has come to signify redemption in Christ. It teaches justification, the work that Christ has done for us, and sanctification, what He is doing in us. The Sabbath testifies to the complete redemptive activity of our Lord.

In the Deuteronomic version of the fourth commandment, the Israelites were told to keep the Sabbath as a remembrance of their escape from slavery in Egypt (see Deuteronomy 5). Thus Sabbath, besides signifying Creation, signifies freedom, redemption, and deliverance through Jesus as well.

As a sign of justification, the Sabbath shows our utter dependence on God for salvation. On the Sabbath we rest from our own works, trusting instead in His works for us. On the Creation Sabbath, our parents had no works to offer God. All they could do was to rest in His creative acts for them. We are in a similar position, relying now not only on God's creative works but on His redemptive ones as well.

"The Sabbath, when understood as that which strips us of

116

our works and our autonomy before God," writes Sakae Kubo, "cannot be used as a means of self-justification. Its very nature militates against its being used in such a way. The Sabbath is truly the sign of God's grace and sovereignty and of man's receptivity and dependence."[72]

The Sabbath signifies also God's creative power working to renew us. " 'Moreover I also gave them My Sabbaths, to be a sign between them and Me, that they might know that I am the Lord who sanctifies them' " (Ezekiel 20:12). Jesus wants not only to forgive us, He wants to change us, to make us new people, which is why He declared, " 'You must be born again' " (John 3:7). Rebirth implies a creative process that only the Lord can provide.

"Therefore, if anyone is in Christ, he is a new creation; old things have passed away; behold, all things have become new" (2 Corinthians 5:17). "And be renewed in the spirit of your mind, and . . . put on *the new man* which was created according to God, in righteousness and true holiness" (Ephesians 4:23, 24, emphasis supplied).

The Sabbath symbolizes not only the created world, but the soul re-created in Christ. Christians who properly keep the Sabbath openly acknowledge the dual role of grace both to forgive and to cleanse the sinner committed to Christ.

40

"Time," William Carlos Williams writes, "is a storm in which we all are lost."

If true, then Sabbath is the compass by which we regain our bearings, because it points us to the One who owns not only space but time as well. By keeping the Sabbath we acknowledge that God is sovereign over not only every atom, but every moment. Thus, time becomes, not as Tennyson wrote, "a maniac spreading dust," but a gift from God, and by keeping His Sabbath we worship that Giver, the true God.

From the first week in Eden, Sabbath has signified worship of the Creator, the true God. Indeed, worship has always been a crucial factor in the faith of God's people, and the book of Revelation teaches that prior to Christ's second coming, it will be so again.

According to John, the "beast," an apostate church-state regime (in Bible prophecy, animals symbolize political powers), will force the world to "*worship* the image of the beast" (Revelation 13:15, emphasis supplied). This means that people will be coerced into paying homage to an aspect of this beast's power. In contrast, an angel from heaven calls for mankind to " '*worship* Him who made heaven and earth, the sea and springs of water' "—the Creator, the true God (Revelation 14:7, emphasis supplied). This angel's call reflects the language of the fourth commandment, which acknowledges Him who " 'made the heavens and the earth, the sea, and all that is in them,' " again, the Creator, the true God (Exodus 20:11).

Those who refuse to worship the beast, worshiping the Lord instead, are described as keeping " 'the commandments of God and the faith of Jesus' " (Revelation 14:12). Because the Sabbath is the only one of the "commandments of God" that specifically points to the Lord as Creator and to His creative power as the reason He should be worshiped, many believe that the fourth commandment will be a vital factor in this final conflict over worship.

Of course, saintly Christians have kept Sunday throughout history. Many do today. We worship a God who loves and accepts us despite our mistakes—a God who saves us, not according to our knowledge, but according to His grace.

God loves those who keep Sunday as much as He does those who keep Sabbath. The question regarding Sabbath is not about God's love for us, but about our love for God. Do we love Jesus enough that when new light comes, we will follow it—not to be saved, but because we already have been saved?

"This is the love of God, that we keep His commandments" (1 John 5:3), and one of His commandments reads that "the *seventh* day"—not the third, first, or fourth—"is the Sabbath of the Lord your God" (Exodus 20:10, emphasis supplied). No matter how many people have sincerely kept or keep Sunday, no matter the blessings Sunday has brought, no matter how deeply entrenched Sunday is in Christianity, Sunday keeping is not obedience to God but obedience to a commandment of men. Jesus warned: " 'In vain they worship Me, teaching as doctrines the commandments of men' " (Matthew 15:9).

41

Imagine a vast, pulsating throng composed of those who, throughout history, have kept Sunday. Besides the unknown millions, church fathers such as Clement of Alexandria, Origen, Ignatius, and Justin Martyr are there. Amid the mass stand the great and revered—Saint Augustine, Saint Francis, and Saint Thomas Aquinas, popes, cardinals, monks, and many selfless missionaries who devoted, even donated, their lives to spread the gospel. Martin Luther, John Calvin, William Wilberforce, John Wesley, Charles Finney, William Miller, and Charles Spurgeon stand among them, along with Mother Teresa, Pope John Paul II, and even Billy Graham.

Another group, smaller, lowlier, and more meek than the first, has gathered nearby. It is composed of those who have kept the seventh-day Sabbath. Because " 'the Sabbath was made for man' " (Mark 2:27), Adam, the first man, stands there. Abraham, who " 'obeyed My voice and kept My charge, My commandments, My statutes, and My law' " (Genesis 26:4, 5), stands with this group too, along with Moses, Aaron, King David, John the Baptist, John the Revelator, Paul, James, and Peter. Throughout history, in Asia, Europe, and Africa, there have been scattered Christians who, despite persecutions, alienation, and suffering, have kept the seventh-day Sabbath, sometimes at the cost of their lives. They are numbered among this group too. Standing also in the crowd are those Christians from almost every land today who, though unable to boast the big names or numbers of their Sunday-keeping contemporaries, keep the seventh-day Sabbath.

Yet one more person remains. He who spoke His holy day into existence, who thundered it from Sinai, who called Himself the Lord of the Sabbath, stands meek and lowly amid that smaller, less-imposing throng. Then, extending His scarred hands as if to embrace His flock in both groups, Jesus pulls in His breath and in a loving plea that has echoed across the millennia cries out, " 'If you love Me, keep My commandments' " (John 14:15)!

Endnotes

1. Eugene Peterson, "Confessions of a Former Sabbath Breaker," *Christianity Today*, 2 September 1988, p. 25.

2. Walter Chantry, *Call the Sabbath a Delight* (Carlisle, Pa.: The Banner of Truth, 1991), p. 12.

3. Frederick Harris, "The Sabbath Was Made for Mankind," in *The Lord's Day*, ed. James P. Wesberry (Nashville: Broadman Press, 1986), p. 77.

4. Ellen White, *The Desire of Ages* (Mountain View, Calif.: Pacific Press, 1940), p. 289.

5. Quoted from a pamphlet by the Lord's Day Alliance, "Scripture I Hardly Noticed" (Atlanta: Lord's Day Alliance of the United States).

6. James P. Wesberry, "Remember the Lord's Day to Keep It Holy," *Sunday*, July-September 1989, p. 4.

7. George Elliott, *The Abiding Sabbath* (1884), pp. 17, 18, quoted in Samuele Bacchiocchi, *Divine Rest for Human Restlessness* (Berrien Springs, Mich.: Biblical Perspectives, 1980), p. 70.

8. Quoted in Wesberry, ed., *The Lord's Day*, p. 51.

9. Marva Dawn, *Keeping the Sabbath Wholly* (Grand Rapids, Mich.: William B. Eerdmans, 1989), p. 9.

10. Samuele Bacchiocchi, *Divine Rest for Human Restlessness* (Berrien Springs, Mich.: Biblical Perspectives, 1980), p. 93.

11. Abraham Joshua Heschel, *The Sabbath* (New York: Farrar, Straus, Giroux, 1983), p. 90.

12. Bacchiocchi, *Divine Rest*, p. 94.

13. Karl Barth, *Church Dogmatics*, vol. 3, part 2 (McLean, Va.: Books International), p. 62.

14. See Clifford Goldstein, *Bestseller* (Boise, Idaho: Pacific Press, 1989).

15. Bacchiocchi, *Divine Rest*, p. 201.

16. Chantry, *Call the Sabbath a Delight*, p. 96.

17. James P. Wesberry, "Let the Trumpet Sound," *Sunday*, Centennial Edition, 1988, p. 5.

18. Dawn, *Keeping the Sabbath Wholly*, p. xi.

19. Alphabet of Rabbi Akiba, *Otzar Midrashim*, p. 407.

20. Al Nakawa, *Menorat* ha-Maor, vol. 2, p. 182, quoted in Heschel, *The Sabbath*, p. 19.

21. Heschel, *The Sabbath*, p. 8.

22. James Brown, "The Doctrine of the Sabbath in Karl Barth's *Church Dogmatics*," *Scottish Journal of Theology*, 20 (1967), p. 7. Quoted in Bacchiocchi, *Divine Rest*, p. 279.

23. Harold Dressler, "The Sabbath in the Old Testament," in *From Sabbath to Lord's Day*, ed. D. A. Carson (Grand Rapids, Mich.: Zondervan, 1982), p. 23.

24. Martin Buber, *Moses: The Revelation and the Covenant* (New York: Oxford University Press, 1946), pp. 84, 85.

25. White, *The Desire of Ages*, p. 283.

26. Gerhard Hasel, "The Sabbath in the Pentateuch," in *The Sabbath in Scripture and History*, ed. Kenneth Strand (Washington, D.C.: Review and Herald Publishing Association, 1982), p. 27.

27. Buber, *Moses*, p. 80.

28. Translated from *Auslegung des Alten Testaments* (Commentary on the Old Testament) in *Sammtliche Schriften* (Collected Writings), ed. J. G. Walch, vol. 3, col. 950, quoted in *Bible Readings for the Home*, p. 304.

29. Chantry, *Call the Sabbath a Delight*, p. 101.

30. Jacques Doukhan, "Loving the Sabbath as a Christian," in *The Sabbath in Jewish and Christian Traditions*, ed. Tamara Eskenazi, Daniel J. Harrington, and William Shea (New York: Crossroad Publishing Co., 1991), p. 159.

31. Roy Branson, ed., *Festival of the Sabbath* (Takoma Park, Md.: Association of Adventist Forums, 1985), p. 72.

32. Ahad Ha-'Am, "The Sabbath Has Kept Israel," in *Sabbath: Day of Delight*, ed. Abraham E. Millgram (Philadelphia: Jewish Publication Society of America, 1944), p. 253.

33. Walter Harrelson, *The Ten Commandments and Human Rights* (Philadelphia: Fortress Press, 1980), p. 82.

34. *Shabbath* 22:1.

35. *Eccl*. R. 5:10:2.

36. *Shabbath* 13:5-7.

37. *Shabbath* 1:3.

38. *Betzah* 1:1.

39. *Shabbath* 21:1.

40. *Shabbath* 7:2.

41. Strand, ed., *The Sabbath in Scripture*, p. 105.

42. Matthew 12:9; Mark 1:21; 3:1; 6:2; Luke 6:6.

43. D. A. Carson, "Jesus and the Sabbath in the Four Gospels," in *From Sabbath to Lord's Day*, ed. D. A. Carson (Grand Rapids, Mich.: Zondervan, 1982), p. 61.

44. Ibid.

45. Strand, ed., *The Sabbath in Scripture*, p. 95.

46. Theodore Friedman, "The Sabbath: Anticipation of Redemption," *Judaism* 16, 1967, p. 443.

47. *Shabbath* 12a.

48. Jacob Jervell, *Luke and the People of God* (Minneapolis, 1972), p. 140.

49. Strand, ed., *The Sabbath in Scripture*, p. 103.

50. Carson, *From Sabbath to Lord's Day*, p. 85.

51. Carson, ibid, back cover.

52. Augustus Neander, *The History of the Christian Religion and Church* (1831), vol. 1, p. 337, quoted in Bacchiocchi, *From Sabbath to Sunday*, p. 108.

53. F. W. Grosheide, *Commentary on the First Epistle to the Corinthians, The New International Commentary on the New Testament*, ed. Ned Stonehouse (Grand Rapids, Mich.: William B. Eerdmans, 1953), p. 398.

54. Strand, ed., *The Sabbath in Scripture*, p. 125.

55. Wesberry, ed., *The Lord's Day*, p. 100.

56. Ibid., p. 239.

57. Carson, ed., *From Sabbath to Lord's Day*, p. 16.

58. James P. Wesberry, "Are We Compromising Ourselves?" *Sunday*, April-June 1976, p. 5.

59. Harold Lindsell, "Consider the Case for Quiet Saturdays," *Christianity Today*, 5 November 1976, p. 42.

60. Strand, ed., *The Sabbath in Scripture*, p. 11.

61. Flavius Josephus, *Against Apion* 2.40, quoted in Abraham Millgram, *Sabbath: Day of Delight* (Philadelphia: Jewish Publica-

tion Society of America, 1981), p. 218.

62.   Adam Clarke, *The New Testament of Our Lord and Savior Jesus Christ* (New York, n.d.), vol. 2, p. 524, quoted in Strand, ed., *Sabbath in Scripture and History*, p. 340.

63.   Carson, ed., *From Sabbath to Lord's Day*, pp. 198-220.

64.   Samuele Bacchiocchi, *The Sabbath in the New Testament* (Berrien Springs, Mich.: Biblical Perspectives, 1985), pp. 79-85.

65.   Samuele Bacchiocchi, *Anti-Judaism and the Origin of Sunday* (Rome: Pontifical Gregorian University Press, 1975), p. 58.

66.   Samuele Bacchiocchi, *From Sabbath to Sunday* (Rome: Pontifical Gregorian University Press, 1977), p. 185.

67.   Rev. Peter Geiermann, *The Convert's Catechism of Catholic Doctrine*, 2nd ed. 1910, p. 50, quoted in Mark Finley, *The Forgotten Day* (Arkansas: The Concerned Group, Inc., 1988), p. 99.

68.   *The Catholic Mirror*, 23 September 1893, quoted in *Rome's Challenge* (Washington, D.C.: International Religious Liberty Association), p. 24.

69.   Strand, ed., *Sabbath in Scripture*, p. 302.

70.   Branson, ed., *Festival of the Sabbath*, p. 47.

71.   Robert Shuler, *God's Everlasting Sign*, p. 90, quoted in *Seventh-day Adventists Believe . . .* (Silver Spring, Md.: Ministerial Association, General Conference of Seventh-day Adventists, 1988), p. 265.

72.   Branson, ed., *Festival of the Sabbath*, p. 44.

If you enjoyed this book . . .

and would like to receive additional materials or information, simply indicate your choices, print your name and address, then tear out this page and mail it to:

A Pause for Peace
P.O. Box 7000
Boise, ID 83707

_____ I would like to purchase a copy of ***The Desire of Ages***, the classic book on the life of Christ. (Enclose check or money order for $3.50, payable to Pacific Press.)

_____ I would like a **FREE** set of Bible study guides.

_____ I would like information concerning a free seminar on the book of Revelation in my area.

_____ I would like a list of other books published by Pacific Press.

_____ I would like **FREE** information on other literature related to the topics contained in this book.

(These offers good in the United States and Canada only.)

_____

For further information, call toll free:
Adventist Information Services
1-800-253-3000.